I1
CHRISTMAS

An Irish Christmas

Stephen Newman

In memory of my mother, Joan Newman

First published 2016

The History Press Ireland
50 City Quay
Dublin 2
Ireland
www.thehistorypress.ie

The History Press Ireland are a member of Publishing Ireland,
the Irish Book Publisher's Association.

British Library Cataloguing in Publication Data.
A catalogue record for this book is available from the British Library.

ISBN 978 1 84588 278 5

Typesetting and origination by The History Press

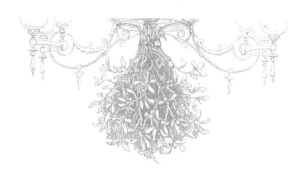

Contents

	Introduction	7
one	Preparation and Decoration	11
two	Christmas Eve	35
three	Christmas Day	73
four	St Stephen's Day and the Day of the Holy Innocents	93
five	The New Year and Epiphany	108
	Notes	138
	Acknowledgements	143

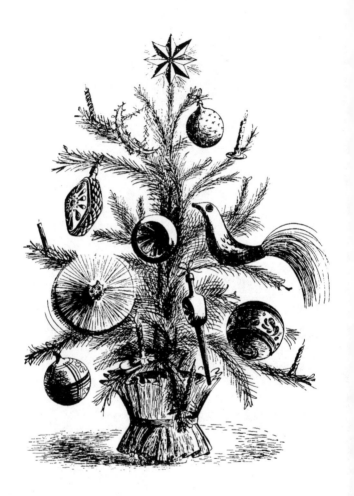

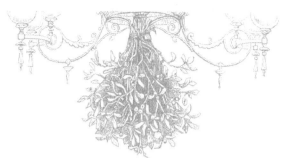

Introduction

The importance of the material contained within the archives of the National Folklore Collection is immense. It is a window into so many aspects of Ireland's cultural history. One aspect of modern Irish consciousness which is highlighted by engagement with the archive is our cultural amnesia. We are disconnected through loss from the customs and beliefs of previous generations. Cultural amnesia is due to various factors, many of which began to gain momentum from the middle part of the nineteenth century. Language shift and other cultural forces associated with colonialism contributed greatly to this amnesia. Other agents of change include the centralization of the Church, which led to the displacement of traditional beliefs, generational changes in the socio-economic standards of families and communities, as well as the multi-faceted forces of globalisation, largely associated with the twentieth century. At the core of the work of what was originally founded as the Folklore of Ireland Society in 1927 (the government established the Irish Folklore Commission in 1935)[1] was the preservation of material from a generation deemed to be one of the last with close links to what was understood as traditional society.

The material on Christmas is extensive and appears in two forms. Firstly, the general accounts of Irish rural life which were collected from the mid-1920s from informants in their sixties and older contain references to Christmas traditions. When reading the accounts by these particular informants, the reader can enjoy a sense of immediacy, as the direct transcription preserves their regional dialect and personal speaking styles. In addition, a large amount of material on Christmas can be found in a standardised questionnaire which was distributed to both full-time and part-time collectors in December 1944. In some cases the questionnaire was completed from interviews with individual informants, while in other cases the collectors conducted multiple interviews which they later summarised.

In December 1944, the Honorary Director of the Commission, Séamus Ó Duilearga, issued a letter to the Commission's collectors and contributors. The following is an extract:

This is the first time that a concerted effort is being made in Ireland to gather the traditional lore of Christmas. A

great amount of valuable information is still available in every corner of the land on this important festival. The questionnaires about other festivals such as Martinmas, Samhain (Halloween), St. John's Day, Lughnasa, were productive of a vast body of material, of which we are very proud. We rely upon you to do what lies in your power to make this questionnaire even more successful than any other issued by us hitherto. We should be grateful if, in making enquiries about the subject-matter of this questionnaire, you concentrated especially on the old traditional manner of celebrating Christmas rather than on the more recent innovations (such as Santa Claus, Christmas cards, mistletoe). We shall be grateful, however, for a note regarding the introduction of these in recent decades too. (NFC 1085: 1, letter from Séamus Ó Duilearga, December 1944.)

Interestingly, what Ó Duilearga calls 'the more recent innovations' of Christmas such as the tree, cards and Santa Claus, are described by informants as coming to the fore within the previous forty to sixty years, and the changes can be tracked moving from the east coast to the west.

In this book the material consulted was collected between 1928-1955. In extracting material from the collection I have attempted to show examples of regional diversity in the traditional celebration of Christmas, as well as including material in the Irish language (with translations). This does not, however, imply that the accounts here are in any way exhaustive. It is certain that many localised variations and nuances do not appear. Also, it is not within the parameters of this publication to adequately examine the often far-reaching and ancient origins of the many customs and beliefs; in many cases this may not even be possible. Of course, the collection itself has its own intrinsic limitations, which have inevitably excluded various groups on the island of Ireland. The work of the Commission was ideologically bound up with the State-building and cultural revival of the post-independence period, with its focus being on a particular view, or understanding, of what was meant by Irishness. This directed it, for the most part, towards a rural, Catholic population, within Irish-speaking areas and areas that had been Irish-speaking up to relatively recently. The large urban areas were largely ignored as well as other religious groupings on the island such as Protestants and Presbyterians.

one

Preparation and Decoration

In traditional Irish society the festival of Christmas was seen as the biggest and greatest festival of the year. People began to look forward to Christmas from the period of Advent (beginning on the fourth Sunday before Christmas). It was a time of spiritual preparation; a reflective period during which attention was directed towards the coming of the Christ Child as a saviour, liberator and redeemer. Seán Ó Duinn writes: 'The various texts which we hear in church during Advent express a longing for a saviour and an enlightener, for somebody who will rescue us from our predicament and who will give direction to our lives.'[1] This anticipation of a saviour is expressed in the following account of a traditional prayer said throughout Advent:

The one special prayer I know of for Christmas was one that started on the first night of the month [1 December] and continued right up 'till Christmas Night. 'Twas said fifteen times nightly by everyone to themselves and 'twas always said after rosary. This is it: 'Hail and blessed be the hour and moment when the Son of God was born in a stable at Bethlehem at midnight, to the most pure Virgin Mary. At that same hour and moment, promise my God to hear my prayer and grant my request.' A lot of the older people had long black laces or bits of strong cord with fifteen knots on it, and they used to use it to say the prayer, the same as we count out the rosary on our beads. (NFC 1391: 133; Tadhg Kelly, Kilrush, County Clare. Collector: Seán McGrath, January 1955.)

Liam Danaher, from Athea, County Limerick, wrote of the importance of saying as many Paters and Aves[2] as possible in the run up to Christmas:

It was an old custom for some time before Christmas to say as many Paters and Aves as possible. The younger folk were urged to keep a record of the daily number of these prayers said, and some could boast of 5,000 prayers. (NFC 1084: 97; written by Liam Danaher, Athea, County Limerick, 1945.)

By December work on the farm would have declined, with the feeding of animals, now in sheds, being the main task.

In 1936 the Commission received a long account of life on a farm from Seán de Buitléir, of Duncormick, County Wexford. In his accompanying letter he wrote *'Tá sé an-deacair cuimhneamh ar gach rud a dheineann an feirmeoir i rith na bliana ach dheineas é chomh maith agus dob fhéidir liom* [It's very hard to remember everything a farmer does during the year but I've done as best I could]':

December comes at last. This is the month which every boy and girl longs to see, especially the school children. On the farm there is not an extraordinary amount of work done. There is plenty of beet seen growing still in the fields. So in this month it is all pulled, and any of it that cannot be got away to the factory is banked out.[3] The marigolds are finished pulling now also, and the farmer starts to pull the turnips. These are pulled in a similar manner as the marigolds, only that they are cleaned well, all the small roots and dirt being cut off. All the turnips are not pulled in this month, but they are pulled as they are wanted. The cows and young cattle are put in the house now about the first day of December, so the work starts again of feeding and minding them. There is some ploughing done and if the weather is fairly fine some winter wheat may be sown, but as a rule coming on to Christmas not much work is done. The farmer may go to a nearby wood and cut down a couple of trees and bring them home for firewood. Another thing that I forgot to mention is the cutting of faggots which takes place in the county. A man goes into a field where there are bushes growing and puts an edge on a bill-hook. Then he puts a 'cuff' on his left hand. This is somewhat like a glove, only it is made of leather. He has the bill-hook in his right hand and the cuff in his left. The first thing that he does is to get two long thin bushes. He catches these in each hand and twists the tops of them into a knot. Then he lays them down on the ground and starts to cut the bushes about the size of a sheaf of corn. He lays this down on the knot of the two bushes. The trick is when there is a weight on the knot it cannot open. Then he cuts another bundle of bushes and places them opposite the other bundle but the butts of both bundles are overlapping. Then he puts on two more bundles in the same manner as described. By this time he has enough cut and laid together and now he sets about tying the faggot. He catches one of the bands and twists it into a loop. Then he gets the far band and pulls it through the loop of the near one, now the far band is twisted and pulled in under the loop of the second one. It is tied in such a way that it cannot be opened. A fairly good man would out about six faggots in the day. These faggots are very handy, for there is no bother loading them. They are used for fencing old gaps. They are also used to roof old sheds that are out in the land for the purpose of sheltering cows etc. (NFC 172: 457–61; written by Seán de Buitléir, Duncormick, County Wexford, March 1936.)

As the festival grew nearer country people headed to the nearest big town to 'bring home the Christmas'. As well as shopping for all the essential supplies, most people speak of getting a 'Christmas box' from some of the shopkeepers in appreciation of their loyalty over the year. The following is from Tone O'Dea of Kilrush, County Clare:

> The country people always did their shopping early in the Christmas and the town's people did too, and they used to say they used to do this simply because they would then get their Christmas boxes from the shop they had been daling[4] in. But there's nothing like them Christmas boxes now. Grocer shops always gave their customers the makings of sweet cakes, a packet of long candles, fruit and maybe a barn brack, then pubs would give a bottle of whiskey when things was cheap, and then they started dolin'[5] out them coloured wines. Every house had four, five, or six dozen of porter in bottles in for callers over the holidays. (NFC 1391: 126; Tone O'Dea, Kilrush, County Clare. Collector: Seán McGrath, January 1955.)

Mrs McCarthy of Enniskean, County Cork, compares the trip to the town of Bandon before Christmas 'long ago' with the time of writing in 1938:

> Mhuise[6] faith alay[7], tis aisy[8] for us to do our bit of Christmas shopping. You'd get Christmas – all the Christmas you'd want for – in every little crossroad shop

now. 'Tisn't like long 'go at all, when we'd go to town for Christmas. 'Twould be no bother for you to get a bottle of whiskey or two for a Christmas box, not to mind candles and currants and cakes – them were good times. They were good on everyone, only for the shopkeeper was doing well, he couldn't give out all the Christmas boxes. All they can give now is a candle or two and a barnbrack, sure they haven't it I suppose. But long 'go too, there wasn't a shopeen[9] at every crossroads and the town shops were doing better. Them times the Saturday before Christmas you couldn't pull your bags through any shops in Bandon. The people used be coming home at dead dark in the night, after being out all day trying to gather up their messages.[10] Sure you could throw a score o' bowls[11] through the streets the Christmas time. All the little shops through the country are taking the trade away from the towns. 'Tis to Bandon I always go for Christmas. I'll have the turkeys out the second Saturday before it. 'Twas always counted on to be the best day for turkeys. Only for the few turkeys faith, we couldn't buy Christmas at all. The bit we'll make out of the cows at this time of year won't do much more than keep the house going for us. (NFC 462: 230; Mrs McCarthy (62), Enniskean, County Cork. Collector: Diarmuid Ó Cruadhlaoich, January 1938.)

The house, both inside and out, was thoroughly cleaned, with walls whitewashed, and the general farmyard area received a good sprucing up. Holly and ivy were the main forms of decorations, with children often sent out to the fields or the woods to collect them. It was generally believed that Christmas decorations should be up by Christmas week. Mrs McCarthy gives an account of these preparations in the lead up to Christmas:

Oh then, the dear knows. It do be running an' racing with us to try an' tidy up the house a bit always for Christmas. With the short days an' all our work, there's a 'fahar'[12] on us to try an' rub a bit a whitewash to the walls, an' up

there around the hob. An' the men if you pulled 'em they couldn't spare time to sweep the chimney for us. You'd think 'twas the harvest was calling 'em outside.

But whatever, anything would do, I'd try and put some bit o' colour on them ould[13] walls.

The dresser an' the ware will want a scrub an' a bit o' tidying up if we can spare time to do it, but we always have a cow or two calving about Christmas an' they must be tended whatever anything else will do. The bit o' butter around Christmas time is worth a bit to us, so we must care the cows anyway. The men will provide a bit of holly an' ivy an' put it up of a night if the fit will take 'em to do it.

It do be put up there all round the dresser, an' around the cupboard, a 'sprig' or two behind the pictures on the walls, a few 'sprigs' here an' there below in the room.

Mhuise, we keeps up the ould custom an' don't take down the holly an' ivy till Shrove Tuesday night an put it bakin' the pancakes.

I don't know, alay, what's the manin[14] of it. I used to see the ould people doin' it an' we're keeping up the ould custom – that's the way with us. (NFC: 462; 228–9; Mrs McCarthy (62), Enniskean, County Cork. Collector: Diarmuid Ó Cruadhlaoich, January 1938.)

The following is a description of the preparations around the house from Mary Walshe and Batt Shea, of Kilrush, County Clare:

Always in the country the outside and inside of the house used to be whitewashed, and the flag floors scrubbed clean for the Christmas. The women did most of this work, and many a woman herself did the whitewashing. Four pence worth of lime, and a ball of blue,[15] added to sour milk, gave the best whitewash of all, and it lasted too, on the walls. In the town, they used always give the windows a special cleaning for Christmas, and the kitchens of every house shone like new pins. Holly was put up either on the day before Christmas Eve itself, or if there was a Sunday near to Christmas Eve, 'twas that day they used to fix the bits of red berry holly over pictures on the mantelpiece, and around the jam-crocks into which they used to put the long Christmas candles. Red berry holly was the favourite, but you had to be sure that none of the berries fell off the holly before Christmas, as if they did, it meant that the birds would pick up the fallen berries, and it meant a death in the house before next Christmas came around. All the people around, when they used to get their *bearts*[16] of holly used to put it in a safe place like up in the attic or in one of the bedrooms, as then it couldn't be out in the open, and there was no chance of it getting picked. A lot of people used to bless the holly the minute they got it, with holy water, as this protected it. Some people used to mix the laurel leaves with the holly, but this was not supposed to be proper. (NFC 1391: 124–5; Mrs Mary Walshe/Batt Shea, Kilrush, County Clare. Collector: Seán McGrath, January 1955.)

The following account of the preparations comes from
north-west Donegal:

*Ní raibh meas ar bith ar aol na cloiche fá choinne na hócáide
seo, ach rachadh achan fhear síos go dtí an trá agus bhéarfadh
siad aníos lód nó ualach sligeán, agus dhófadh siad iad sin agus
bhíodh an t-aol acu a ba ghile agus ab fhéidir a fháil. Nífeadh
fear an tí nó fear inteacht de na buachaillí na ballaí agus nuair
a bheas sin déanta acu bhéarfadh siad a ndícheall cuidiú do
fhear an tí, nó do na cailíní, a ghlanfadh lorg an aoil de na
dorsa agus den urlár. Dhéanfadh siad an níochán seo cúpla lá
roimh Throscadh Oíche Nollag. Ansin rachadh siad go dtí na
beanntáin agus na gleanntáin thart fán áit, agus bhainfeadh
siad ualach mór cuilinn. Dhéanfadh siad faichill mhaith i
gcónaí an cuileann a fháil a mbeadh na blátha beaga deasa
dearga orthu. Bhéarfadh siad ualach maith den eidheann
isteach de na beanna ar an dóigh chéanna. Chóireodh siad agus
ghléasfadh siad suas an teach agus na bóithigh agus na sciobóil
leis an dá chuid. Pictiúirí beannaithe, nó pictiúirí athar nó
máthar, nó den teaghlach a bheadh marbh nó ar shiúil in áit ar
bith, gheibheadh siad san a gcuid féin don chuileann.*

*D'fhágtaí na blátha seo thuas ar na ballaí go dtí Achar
an Dá Lá Dhéag. Lá thar na bhárach i ndiaidh an lae sin,
bhéarfadh siad leobhtha a gcuid stóltaí nó dréimirí agus
leagfadh siad anuas na blátha seo uilig go léir.*

*Níor chuala mé ariamh go raibh leigheas ar bith ins na
blátha seo a bhíos thart ar na ballaí fán Nollaig, nó go mbaintí*

úsáid ar bith astu in éadan pisreogaí nó rud ar bith mar sin.
An té nach gcuirfeadh aol ar a theach faoi Nollaig bheifí ag
ceapadh gur cineál págánach é.

[People hadn't any time for limestone when it came to
the occasion of Christmas. Instead, the men would bring
a load of shells from the beach and melt them, the result
being the brightest lime you could find. The man of the
house, or one of the boys, would clean the walls and when
this was done he would help the man of the house or the
girls to clean the lime marks from the doors and the floor.
They would do this cleaning a couple of days before the
Christmas Eve fast. After this they would head for the
hilltops and glens around about and gather a fine load of
holly. They would always take care to find holly full of red
berries, and they'd always bring back plenty of ivy as well.
They would decorate the house, and the sheds and the barn
with both. Holy pictures, pictures of a father, or mother, or
any member of the household who was deceased, or living
abroad, were decorated with their own piece of holly.

The foliage was left in place until 6 January. The
following day, they would pull out their stools and
ladders and remove the holly and ivy. It was never said
that the foliage on the walls at Christmas held any
medicinal properties, and it was never used for protection
against any superstitions or anything like that. Anyone
who didn't whitewash their house for Christmas was
considerered some sort of pagan.] (NFC 932; 381–2;

Niall Ó Dubhthaigh (69) – with help from his sister
Eibhlín, Cloughaneely, County Donegal. Collector: Seán
Ó hEochaidh, 1943.)

Pàdraic Ó hAichir collected the following from the Aran
Islands:

*Ba ghnáthach i gcónaí, agus gnáthach fós le daoine, na
tithe a mhaisiú le haghaidh na Nollag, istigh agus amuigh,
fiú na cróite. An té nach gcuirfeadh aol ar a theach faoi
Nollaig bheifí ag ceapadh gur cineál págánach é. Ghlanfaí
na sráideanna agus na cosáin le spáid agus scuab agus ní
bheadh siad sásta go gcuirfí gaineamh garbh nó gairbhéal
mín ar na sráideanna agus na cosáin i gCill Rónáin.
Déantar an rud céanna ins na bailtí eile ar fud an oileáin leis
an ngairbhéal mín is gaire dóibh. Faigheann an teach an
glanadh taobh istigh freisin. Cuirtear aol ar na ballaí, glantar
na simléys, sciúrtar na cathaoireacha, stólta agus troscán
eile. Tá an obair seo déanta ar feadh na seachtaine roimh an
Nollaig. Ar an 24ú baintear eidheann, cuileann agus cuirtear
suas ins an gcisteanaigh iad; ar chúl na bpictiúirí, ar an
dreisiúr agus mórán chuile áit arbh fhéidir craobh a chrochadh.
Cuirtear páipéar daite timpeall na bhfuinneog agus timpeall
na gcoinnleoirí. Fadó, déarfaí paidir le linn iad seo a chur suas
agus na coinnlí á lasadh acht ní abraítear aon phaidir anois.*

    *Ba ghnáthach le daoine san oileán seo stuif a cheannach
roimh an Nollaig. Gheibhfeadh daoine an stuif díreach ó*

Ghaillimh. 'Prog na Nollag' a thugtar fós ar an stuif sin. Cheannaíodh siad plúr, tae, siúcra, rísíní, cuiríní, spís, bagún agus amantaí buidéal uisce beatha nó 'special' agus bhí poitín fairsing san seanshaol ins na síbíní. Ba mhaith leo freisin éadach nua eicínt a cheannach le haghaidh Lá Nollag (caipín nó hata, veist nó bróga).

[It was the custom, and still is, that the houses were decorated, both inside and out, for Christmas, even the outhouses were decorated. Anyone who didn't whitewash their house at Christmas was seen as some sort of pagan. The streets and footpaths used to be cleaned with a spade and a brush and they wouldn't be happy until they'd put rough sand or smooth gravel on the streets and footpaths of Kilronan. The same is done in other towns around the island with whatever smooth gravel they find near them. The walls are whitewashed, the chimneys cleaned, chairs, stools and any other furniture is scrubbed. This work is done during the week before Christmas. On 24 December, the ivy and holly is picked and put up around the kitchen, behind pictures, on the dresser, and in almost any spot where a branch could be hung. Coloured paper is put around the windows and around the candle-holders. Long ago a prayer would be said while they were hanging the ivy and the holly, and again while the candles were being lit, but no prayers are said now.

It was the custom for people on the Island to buy supplies before Christmas. They used to get supplies

directly from Galway. This supply is still known as the 'Christmas Prog'. They used to buy flour, tea, sugar, raisins, currants, spice, bacon and sometimes a bottle of whiskey or 'special' and poteen was widespread in the old days in the shebeens.[17] They also liked to buy some new item of clothing for Christmas Day (a cap or a hat, a waistcoat or shoes).] (NFC 1089: 10–1; written by Pádraic Ó hAichir, Kilronan, Aran, County Galway, March 1945.)

Mrs Hanratty from South Armagh, aged 90 in 1944, also speaks of the pre-Christmas visit to town, and describes how they decorated the house when she was a child:

Well, indeed, everyone would go out to the town for the Christmas things. The Marragamore[18] they called it indeed. Them up on the mountain would be waitin' down on the road for hours for the carts goin' [to get a lift]. 'Humpy Thursday' they called it; everybody would be carryin' baskets and loads on their backs. Indeed, I seen[19] lines of creels[20] from Omeath (County Louth) an' everywhere in Newry on Humpy Thursdays. The people bought all they could. I mind a wee lassie[21] that was here an' her waitin' for them to come home, an' the first thing she said when the parents come into the street was: 'Da! Have you the cow's head?' Everyone would try to have one.

They would decorate the house with holly and ivy, and some would put up coloured paper. It's not a saint then

be's[22] on the thorns of the holly, but an angel I heard. There was no decorating done outside. Well, they might give the house outside a lick of whitewash. And some would put up a bit of holly over the door outside. Holly was hard to get in them days. It's hard to grow it. It's plentiful now. I'd be going out to Dundalk in the cart, and there'd be hedges of holly growing up be[23] Matt McElroys [on the border of Louth and Armagh, at Carrickasticken, Dromintee] And away up be Bradford's. (NFC 1087: 124–5; Bridget Hanratty (90), Dromintee, County Armagh. Collector: Michael J. Murphy, December 1944.)

While there are many accounts relating to the food that was bought and prepared in the lead up to Christmas, the following account from Niall Ó Dubhthaigh is a rarity in that he includes a reasonably complete recipe for a traditional bread made by his father, who was a baker:

Bhíodh arán deas ag m'athair dúinne i gcónaí le linn na Nollag. Bhí clú mhór aige ar fud an chontae mar fhuinteoir agus mar fhear a bhí ábalta arán milis a dhéanamh, agus bhíodh ráchairt mhór ar a chuid arán ag bodaigh mhóra ins na laethaibh sin. Tchífinn é ag dul síos nuair a bhí mé i mo pháiste agus bhí mórán nithe aige le cur ins an arán seo: Ins an chéad chás de bhéarfadh sé leis builbhín aráin agus scríobhfadh sé síos an builbhín sin go mbeadh sé cóir a bheith chomh mion leis an phlúr aige. Nuair a bheadh sin millte síos aige chomh deas mín agus ab fhéidir é a bheith, gheobhadh sé leath-phunta gearach – geir a bhainfí as

ainmhí caora nó bollóg, Mhillfeadh sé seo leis an scríobán ar an dóigh chéanna; an gheir chomh mín agus ab fhéidir. Gheibheadh sé punta siúcra ansin agus chuireadh sé isteach ins an mhias é ar an dóigh chéanna. Gheibheadh sé punta rísíní ansin, agus ceithre unsa de lemon peel, agus sin a ghearradh chomh mion agus ab fhéidir ar chlár le scian mhaith ghéar. Gheibheadh sé ansin dhá unsa spice agus chuireadh sé fríd an iomlán é. Bheireadh sé leis leath-phunta de phrátaí bruite ansin agus bhruitheadh sé iad agus chuireadh sé isteach ins an scála iad nuair a bhíodh siad bruite go mion aige, agus ansin ar mhullach an iomláin. Chuirfeadh sé síos tuairim ar leath-unsa salainn. Dhéanfadh sé sin a oibriú go ndéanfadh sé taos de. Bheadh sé deacair a dhéanamh nó bhí na rudaí a d'ainmnigh mé uilig an-bhrisc. Ghlacadh sé leathuair mhaith ar a laghad an méid a bheadh ins an mhias a oibriú ar scor a dhéanamh mar ba chóir. Nuair a bhíodh sé oibrithe go maith ansin aige d'fhágadh sé sa mhias é go dtí go n-éiríodh sé cruaidh. Chaitheadh sé toiseacht air ansin arís agus á dhéanamh cruinn sa chruth go mbíodh sé réidh lena bhruith. Chuireadh sé isteach in éadach ansin é. Dhéanfadh ceannadhart, nó a leithéid sin, cúis agus sreangán beag a theannadh thart ar a bhéal.

Bheadh pota uisce ar an tine ansin aige agus chuireadh sé síos ins an phota é ansin. Chuireadh sé síos ar an tine é ansin ar feadh sé huaire, agus ar feadh an ama sin bhíodh craos tine leis i rith an ama. Chaithfí tine mhaith a choinneáil leis an phota ar feadh na sé huaire ar scor é a bheith bruite ar an dóigh cheart. Bhí sin ar phroinn chomh blasta agus a bhlais duine ar bith ariamh.

[My father always used to have lovely bread for us during Christmas. He was well known as a baker all over the county and as a man well able to produce a fine sweet bread. There was great demand for his bread among the bigwigs of the area in those days. I would see him at work when I was a child and a lot of ingredients went into this bread. Firstly, he'd take a loaf of bread and he'd grate it until it was almost as fine as the flour. When he'd have all that grated down as smooth as can be, he would add a half-pound of fat from either a sheep or a bullock. He'd grate that down in the same way, making the fat as smooth and fine as possible. He'd get a pound of sugar then and add it to the dish in the same way. He'd then add a pound of raisins and four ounces of lemon peel, and he'd chop it up finely with a good sharp knife. He'd then add two ounces of spice to the mix. He'd boil a half-pound of potatoes and once they were well boiled he'd add them to the bowl, placing them on top of the mix. He'd add about a half-ounce of salt to the bowl. He'd work it into a dough. It would be hard to do this because all the ingredients I mentioned were brittle. He used to spend at least half an hour working the bowl until he got it right. Once he was satisfied he used to leave it sit in the bowl until it hardened. He used to start on it again and get it into a shape ready for cooking. He then used to place it inside a cloth – the likes of a pillow case would do fine, with the opening tied with string. He'd have a pot of water on the fire and he'd

then place it in the pot and leave it on a roaring fire for six hours. A good fire would have to be kept going for the six hours if it was going to be cooked properly. That was one of the tastiest meals a person could have.] (NFC 932: 393–5, Niall Ó Dubhthaigh (69) – with help from his sister Eibhlín, Cloughaneely, County Donegal. Collector: Seán Ó hEochaidh, 1943.)

The origins of mumming and the Mummers' plays are still not completely understood, though their emergence in Ireland is almost certainly of English origin. The tradition is associated with certain areas; Wexford, Dublin, and the northern counties have strong traditions. The plays often feature notable figures from history or mythology. Kevin Danaher describes the characters in a Mummers' play from County Wexford.

In a Wexford Mummers' play, composed about the beginning of the century, all the characters are from Irish history, Colmcille, Brian Boru, Art McMorrough, Owen Roe O'Neill, Sarsfield, Wolfe Tone, Lord Edward, Kelly of Killane, Michael Dwyer, Robert Emmet and Father John Murphy, all led by the captain who calls on each to speak his lines. Wexford mumming differs from all the others in that the highlight of the performance is an intricate sword dance. There are always twelve players each with a wooden sword.[24]

Mummers' plays were often performed in the days leading up to Christmas. Niall Ó Dubhthaigh gives quite a comprehensive account of the Mummers and their customs from his own part of north-west Donegal:

Bhíodh gleo mór cinnte ag an mhuintir óg ar feadh dóigh anseo thart fá laethaibh na Nollag. B'fhéidir go gcruinneodh cúig nó sé déag de chloigne acu dó nó trí oícheannaí roimh Oíche Nollag Mór, agus rachadh siad amach fríd an tír lena gcuid ranntaí. B'fhéidir go mbeadh siad i rith seachtaine nó níos mó ná sin ag foghlaim na ranntaí seo, agus nuair a bhíodh siad ag dul amach ar an dóigh seo bhíodh éide galánta as miosúr orthu. Ins an am a bhfuil mé ag trácht air, ba é sin an t-éide a chaitheadh na buachaillí thart anseo: brístí geala muilscín, agus bhíodh siad sin chomh geal le heala na toinne. Ní raibh buachaill ar bith ag dul isteach thíos anseo i dteach pobail Ghort a' Choirce in m'óigse nárbh é sin an sórt brístí a bhí siad á gcaitheamh uilig go léir, agus ar an ócáid seo thart fán Nollaig, bheadh na brístí geala muilscín seo orthu agus léinteacha geala úra amach as an tsiopa; léinteacha línéadaigh agus iad sin taobh amuigh dá gcuid éadaigh. Ansin, ghníodh siad féin hataí páipéir, agus chuireadh na cailíní cuid mhór ribín glas agus dearg, agus achan rud ba dheise ná a chéile.

Bhí claidheamh maide ansin ag achan fhear acu. An buachaill a bheadh dea-lámhach, dhéanfadh sé na claidheacha seo don scaifte uilig. D'imeodh siad ar maidin nó teacht an lae dá mbeadh siad ag dul ar thuras fada, agus

*ní stopfadh siad b'fhéidir, go mbeadh siad thiar i bparóiste
Ghaoth Dobhair. Char chuala mé muintir na háite seo ariamh
ag tabhairt ainm ar bith ar na buachaillí seo a théadh amach
mar seo ach na Mummers. Bhéarfadh siad an chéad iarraidh
ar na tithe móra, tithe a mbeadh siad ag meas go raibh
an mhuintir a bhí ina gcónaí iontu go neamhbhuartha
air, agus a raibh airgead acu. Rachadh siad go dtí an doras
ansin agus thosódh siad ar a gcuid ranntaí. Bhíodh scuab
leis an gcéad fhear a tháinig go dtí an doras agus rachadh
seisean isteach an chéad uair chun tí. Chomh luath agus a
rachadh seisean isteach thar an doras bhéarfadh sé thart
an scuab fríd an teach, agus thosódh sé ar an rann seo
aige féin:*

Room, room my gallant boys,
Give us room to rhyme
Till I show you some activity about the Christmas time.
I feel young and active,
and I can act that which was never acted on a stage.
Money I want and money I crave,
And if I don't get money I'll sweep ye all to the grave.

[The young people used to make plenty of noise around
here during the days of Christmas. Maybe about fifteen or
sixteen of them would gather two or three nights before
Christmas Eve, and head off through the country with
their rhymes. They might spend a week or more learning

the rhymes and when they headed out, they dressed in the most exquisite clothes. In the days I'm describing, boys wore the following clothes: bright moleskin trousers as white as a swan on the wave. In my youth, not a single boy went to the church in Gortahork without wearing these white moleskin trousers. They also wore brand new white shirts from the shop; these were linen shirts and were worn outside their clothes. Then they used to make paper hats, and the girls used to hang large green and red ribbons on them, and each one was nicer than the next.

Every man had a wooden sword. A lad who was good with his hands would make the swords for the group. They would leave in the morning or at daybreak if they were going on a long journey, and they might not stop until they were as far as Gweedore. I never heard the people around call these boys by any other name than the Mummers. They'd begin with the big houses, as they thought the residents wouldn't mind and that there'd be money. The first man to the door used to have a brush and he'd be first to enter the house. As soon as he got inside he'd bring the brush through the house and he'd recite the following rhyme:

Room, room my gallant boys,
Give us room to rhyme
Till I show you some activity about the Christmas time.
I feel young and active,

and I can act that which was never acted on a stage.
Money I want and money I crave,
And if I don't get money I'll sweep ye all to the grave.
    (NFC 932: 426–31; Niall Ó Dubhthaigh, Cloghaneely,
    County Donegal. Collector: Seán Ó hEochaidh, 1943.)

Mrs Hanratty of County Armagh shows little regard for the mumming tradition: 'There was no one going about dressed (in disguise) in my time. Is it like Mummers you mane? In troth the people had more sense than to let their children out to a thing like that.' (NFC 1087: 125; Bridget Hanratty (90), Domintee, County Armagh. Collector: Michael J. Murphy, December 1944.)

As Christmas approached those ill or nearing death felt a sense of hope. The following belief was found all over Ireland:

> *Deireadh na seandaoine go mbeadh súil le biseach ag daoine tinn faoi Nollaig. Ba mhaith le seandaoine bás a fháil faoi Nollaig mar deiridís go bhfuil na flaithis oscailte do chuile dhuine an tráth sin.*
>
> [Old people used say the people hoped for an improvement from illness during Christmas. Old people wouldn't mind dying during Christmas as they used to say that heaven is open to all at this time.] (NFC 1089: 14; written by Pádraic Ó hAichir, Kilronan, Aran, County Galway, March 1945.)

The custom of horn blowing in the run up the Christmas is still practiced in the Netherlands. It survives from the period 1500 and is largely associated with Germanic Anglo-Saxon tradition. It is mentioned only once in the material I've examined, in a brief account from Mrs Leonard of Delvin County Westmeath: 'Up to very recent times it was customary in this district to blow horns for some weeks before Christmas to welcome in the feast.' (NFC 1085: 94; Mrs Leonard (94), Delvin, County Westmeath, 1945.)

two

Christmas Eve

Much like present times, it was on Christmas Eve that the festival began in earnest, and this was certainly the most ritualised day of the season. The Christmas story informed most customs, rituals and beliefs, especially as midnight approached, the time when it was believed Jesus was born. Interestingly, the account of Christmas Night, and the birth of Jesus, is relatively short in the New Testament with a far longer description of his death and resurrection. The interaction of the Christmas story with oral tradition has enhanced narrative strands over the centuries and has been continuously retold and reimagined within communities. In her article 'Aifreann na Gine, Aifreann is Fiche',[1] Ríonach Uí Ógáin looks at the richness of lore associated with Christmas Eve. She notes, for example, that the folk imagination in Ireland has had a particularly strong engagement with the image of the Virgin Mary and Joseph seeking shelter in Bethlehem. As we will see, this part of the Christmas story is at the core of the candle rituals and is central to beliefs surrounding charity and generosity.

As families reunite for the festival, the collected material shows that stopping work was taken very seriously. It was almost taboo to engage in anything other than feeding animals and the necessary preparations for the Christmas dinner. All of the twelve days of Christmas were strictly observed as holidays and unnecessary work was commonly suspended until after 6 January. Michael Howard and Thomas Bolger from Kilrush recount the following:

> Neither my three sons nor myself work from the Sunday before Christmas Day until after the Little Christmas. This was always the case amongst the tradesmen of the town. Not alone did painters stop work but also the coopers in Henry Street and the journeymen smiths who used to work at the three Smiths' forges. (NFC 1391: 123; Michael Howard, Thomas Bolger, Kilrush, County Clare. Collector: Seán McGrath, January 1955.)

Niall Ó Dubhthaigh in Donegal emphasises the abstention from work throughout the festival:

CHRISTMAS EVE

Chuala mise m'athair mór á rá gur chuala sé a athair féin á rá ina chuid laethaibh óga san go mbíodh saoire ar an dá lá dhéag sin. Ní bhíodh obair thalamh nó sórt ar bith faoin spéir ag dul anseo nó i bparáiste ar bith eile thart fá dtaobh dúinn Lá Nollag. Bhíodh spórt agus greann agus imirt cluichí agus rudaí mar sin ag dul acu ach ní bheireadh siad arm ar bith ar scor lá oibre a dhéanamh. Bhíodh siad ar shiúil, ag iomání, agus dá mbeadh aonach comhgarach bhíodh siad uilig aige. Bhíodh siad uilig ar shiúil a' seilg fosta. Chasfaí baicle mhór de na buachaillí ar a chéile i mbaile éigin agus bheadh a gcuid cluichí iomána ansin acu agus gach sórt mar sin. Ansin nuair a thiocfadh an oíche bheadh a gcuid céilithe acu ins an chruth go mbeadh sean agus óg páirteach ins an ghreann a bhí ag dul ar aghaidh ar feadh an dá lá dhéag seo. Sin nuair a bhí na laethe glóracha ins an tír seo – i bhfad roimh bhliantaí an drochshaoil. 'Sí bliain an drochshaoil an chéad rud a chuir maide ar an ghnás seo. Nuair a tháinig na bliantaí sin tháinig siad agus chuaigh siad thart agus ní raibh na daoine ariamh ó shoin chomh gleoiréiseach agus a bhí siad roimhe sin.

[I heard my grandfather saying that his own father told him that when he was young the twelve days of Christmas were always a holiday. No work of any sort was done here or in any parish around us during the Christmas period. There used to be sport, merriment and games and so on, but not a tool was lifted to do a day's work. There used to be hurling and if there was a fair anywhere near they used to all attend. They used to go out hunting as well. A gang of boys would meet in some town and have their games of hurling. Then at night they'd have céilí dances, with young and old partaking in the merriment over these twelve days. These were the glory days in this country, long before the famine years. It was the year of the famine that put paid to such customs. These years came and went but the people were never as jolly again as they were before.] (NFC 932: 378–9; Niall Ó Dubhthaigh, Cloghaneely, County Donegal. Collector: Seán Ó hEochaidh, 1943.)

Mrs Bridget Hanratty of south Armagh gives a sense of the taboo surrounding work during Christmas:

Divil[2] the work people done on the twenty-fourth. Not out in the fields. They'd do wee bits of turns about the place (house, yard and haggard[3]). 'Ded,[4] I mind[5] people down the road here who would always start on Christmas Eve, an' divil the much they were better of it. People always remarked it. Lawless they were. They'd start on that day to put out dung. It was always remarked. (NFC 1087: 123–4; Bridget Hanratty (90), Dromintee, County Armagh. Collector: Michael J. Murphy, December 1944.)

The weather would be keenly observed at this time with a number of superstitions surrounding it. The most common in the collection was the following:

They used to say that a 'White Christmas meant a lean churchyard and a Green Christmas meant a fat churchyard.' And 'twas true, as if there was very wet weather around

the Christmas, a lot of people died. And we knew long ago
what sort of weather to expect from the twelve days of the
holidays, as they used to say: 'For each day of Christmas, the
following twelve months will suit.' This meant that each of
the Twelve Days were supposed to represent a month, and
you could reckon on whether the following year would be
wet or fine. (NFC 1391: 123; Tadhg Kelly, Kilrush, County
Clare. Collector: Seán McGrath, January 1955.)

It was not uncommon in Irish folklore to believe that bad
weather was a punishment for the behaviour of humanity
on earth. In the following from Niall Ó Dubhthaigh, he
appears to link the lack of white Christmases to the First
World War (1914–18), which had also contributed to the
general decline in prosperity among the people:

*Tháinig athrach mór ar an Nollaig cinnte ó bhí mise mé féin
óg. Nuair a bhí mé i mo ghasúr agus rachaimís taobh amuigh
den doras, bhíodh an sneachta suas go dtí ár muineál orainn.
Bhíodh achan nduine ag dréim agus bhíodh siad cinnte go
mbeadh sneachta trom ann i dtráthaibh na Nollag. Agus ó
bhí an Cogadh Mór deireanach ann d'imigh an sneachta agus
d'imigh achan rud a raibh rath agus rathúnas ar bith air a
bhaineas leis na daoine nó leis an tír. Tá sé canta ariamh go
ndéan Nollaig ghlas reilig mhéith agus creidim féin go bhfuil
seo fíor go leor. An geimhreadh nach mbíonn an sneachta
ann fán Nollaig, bíonn mórán aicídeacha ag dul agus mórán
daoine, sean agus óg, ag fáil bháis.*

[Christmas has changed so much since I was young. When I was a child you'd go out the door and be up to your neck in snow. Everybody expected snow and were certain of heavy snow around Christmas. But since the last Great War, the snow has left, along with everything that provided wealth and prosperity to either the people or the country. It has always been said that a green Christmas leads to a fat graveyard and I believe this to be true. A Christmas without snow is full of illness, and results in the death of a lot of people, both young and old.] (NFC 932: 385; Niall Ó Dubhthaigh, Cloghaneely, County Donegal. Collector: Séan Ó hEochaidh, 1943.)

One aspect of Christmas Eve that has largely disappeared is the practice of fasting from early that morning until supper is served after dark. Bríghid Ní Aghartaigh, from County Donegal, describes it as follows, as heard from her grandmother: *'Roimhe seo dhéanfadh an lá roimh Lá Nollag a throscadh. Ní íosfaí tadaí an lá sin ach trí ghreim arán coirce agus trí bholgam uisce ar maidin'* [Before now, the day before Christmas Day was always a fast day. Nothing would be eaten apart from three bites of oat bread and three mouthfuls of water]. (NFC 335: 136; Bríghid Ní Aghartaigh (30), Kilcar, County Donegal. Collector: Anna Ní Éigheartaigh, March 1936.)

In Kilrush the day itself was austere, with fasting and confession:

CHRISTMAS EVE

As long as I remember Christmas Eve was always a fast day, and workmen, immediately they finished work at noon, went straight to confession. They had a tea dinner, as they used to call it, tea and bread and jam, when they came home. (NFC 1391: 127; Tone O'Dea, Kilrush, County Clare. Collector: Seán McGrath, January 1955.)

Bríghid Ní Ruairc from County Cork describes the fast and the meal they enjoyed that night:

On Christmas Eve you'd get nothing to eat from breakfast – which was potatoes and dip (dip made of milk, salt and pepper, or usually grey water, salt and pepper, owing to the scarcity of milk) – until about 7pm, when the first supper was served. For this we had potatoes, fish (hake) and sauce made of milk and flour mixed together and boiled. The late supper, about 10.00pm, consisted of bread, butter, tea and currant cake. If any of us fell asleep before the last supper on Christmas Night, my father used say: *'Éirígí as san nó gheobhaidh sibh an mol.'* [Give that up or you will get the 'mol']. The 'mol' was some fine fat sheep they had in heaven. Whiskey, porter and wine were drunk after the last supper. (NFC 1084: 160; Bríghid Ní Ruairc (70), Bantry, County Cork. Collector: Conchubhair Ó Ruairc, 1945.)

In Donegal the evening meal brought the fast to an end:

*Sé an gnás anseo an dinnéar a ithe i dtráthaibh a haon a chlog
sa lá. Ba é an gnás a bhí ann an dinnéar a chur chun moille
go dtí an tráthnóna troscadh Oíche Nollag Mór. D'fhanachtaí
insan am sin leis an chlapsholas go mbeadh achan nduine don
teaghlach sa bhaile. Nuair a shuífí isteach chuig an tsuipéar
ansin, dà mbeadh fear an tí beo choisreodh sé an bia. Cha
raibh paidir nó rud ar bith speisialta aige a déarfadh sé ach go
n-iarrfadh sé ar Dhia gan an teaghlach a laghdú – 'go méadaí
Dia ár gcuid agus ár gcuideachta,' a déarfadh sé. Dá mbeadh
an t-athair marbh nó ar shiúil, 'sí an mháthair nó bean an tí
a déarfadh seo. Idir sin agus an luí bíonn tae agus achan sórt
is fearr ná a chéile ag na daoine anois, ach ins an tseanam, ní
raibh iomrá ar bith ag na créatúir a bhí ann ar an milsíneacht
atá ag dul ar na blianta deireanacha seo anois.*

[The custom here is to eat dinner around one o'clock.
But on Christmas Eve, due to the fast, it was delayed until
evening. We waited until twilight when every member
of the household would be at home. When we'd sit down
to eat, it was the man of the house, if he were still alive,
who would bless the food. There was no special prayer or
words but he would ask God not to take anybody from the
household – 'may God increase our lot and our company,'
he would say. If the father was dead or away, the mother
or the woman of the house would say the prayer. Before
bedtime people have tea and a variety of treats. In the
old days people never heard tell of all the sweet things
available in recent years.] (NFC 932: 399–400; Niall Ó
Dubhthaigh, Cloghaneely, County Donegal. Collector:
Seán Ó hEochaidh, 1943.)

CHRISTMAS EVE

The following account is from Kilronan, on the Aran Islands:

Is lá troscaidh é an 24ú, 'sé sin tá bigil ar an lá ach níl sé dian. Tá dhá shuipéar ins gach teach ar Oíche Nollag; le haghaidh an chéad shuipéir, tar éis na gcoinnlí a lasadh, tá fataí agus iasc, searc úr más féidir ach is annamh is féidir, nó searc saillte, ballach, mangach, bréim nó langa is fearr leo. Ní cheapfaí go mbeadh ronnach saillte sách gnaíúil don ócáid. Cuirtear príáil air nó anlann; tá an príáil déanta as bainne bruite ina mbíonn plúr leáite, oinniún agus gráinne beag siúcra. Fadó, d'ithtí an béile seo thíos ag an tine agus na fataí sa cheiseog agus a phláta féin ag chuile dhuine ar a ghlúinibh. Isteach ag an mbord anois é anseo. Tamall ina dhiaidh sin leagtar an bord i lár urláir na cistine. Bíonn cístí milse déanta le cúpla lá roimhe sin agus cuirtear ar an mbord iad in éindí le subh, im srl. Tá pota mór tae déanta agus ólann agus itheann chuile dhuine a sháith. Roimh an dara suipéar deirtear: 'go mbeirimid beo ar an am seo arís.'

[The 24th is a fast day; there is a vigil but not a strict one. There are two suppers in every house on Christmas Eve. For the first supper, after lighting the candles, there is potatoes and fish, fresh shark if possible, though it rarely is, or salted shark. They prefer wrasse, pollock, bream or tangle. Salted mackerel wouldn't be deemed appropriate for the occasion. A sauce or soup, made from boiled milk mixed with flour, onion and a small grain of sugar, was also served. Long ago this meal was eaten down by the fire, with the potatoes in a basket, and everybody with a

plate on their lap. It is now eaten up at the table. Later, a table is laid in the middle of the floor. Sweet cakes are made a couple of days before and they are placed on the table with jam and butter etc. A big pot of tea is made and everybody eats and drinks their fill. Before the second supper the following is said: 'May we all be alive at this time again.'] (NFC 1089: 10–11; written by Pádraic Ó hAichir, Kilronan, Aran, County Galway, March 1945.)

CHRISTMAS EVE

Mrs Hanratty, in south Armagh, mentions eating 'the champ' on Christmas Eve. She doesn't mention her ingredients but in the north of Ireland it was traditionally made with mashed potato, scallion and butter:

> Christmas Eve was always a fast. No one would touch flesh meat. You'd have champ on Christmas Eve. There was a man here, he had a parish priest a brother, and a well learned man, and he called in here Christmas Eve, and says he: 'Have you the champ out?'
>
> 'I have not,' says I, 'but it's on the fire.'
>
> 'Well,' says he, 'if it's on the fire, I'll wait till it's done.'
>
> He'd only ate a spoonful or two, but it wouldn't look right if you didn't have champ on Christmas Eve. And you would. You'd have hard oatmeal bread. There wasn't much word of tea in the oul' times. There'd be whiskey and drink. The people could get potshin (poteen). It was made in every hole and corner then. (NFC 1087: 124; Bridget Hanratty (90), Dromintee, County Armagh. Collector: Michael J. Murphy, December 1944.)

In many houses the Christmas candles were lit before the meal and this ritual, above all, marked the beginning of the festival. While the lighting of the candles was a ritual in households all over Ireland, there were variations as regards to who lit the candle and also some variations in terms of its meaning and the superstitions surrounding it. The core belief was that the candles represented a welcome for Joseph and Mary as they wandered through Bethlehem in search of shelter. Mrs Mary Walshe describes the importance of Christmas candles during her own childhood:

Indeed then, you have to buy them now, and they cost nine shillings for a packet of twelve, but long ago we used to get them in the box of stuff we got as the Christmas box from the shopkeepers. They were always white and they stood about 20 inches tall. Two were always lighted and left in the kitchen – on the sill of the window, and then there was one lighted and put in every room of the house.

'Twas always my father used to light them and the youngest girl used to have the bottle of holy water in her hand to give him after he lighting them. Then he'd sprinkle the holy water on the candle, and on all of us gathered in the kitchen, and on the walls of the kitchen, and he used to say in Irish 'Go mbeirimid go léir beo ar an am seo arís.' [May we all be alive at this time again.] Then one of the girls would take the candles to their rooms, and my father would spend the night looking and minding them to see they were alright. Three sets of candles were used during the Christmas. The first set were lighted on Christmas Eve, and they were lighted the following two or three nights until they were burned out.

Then New Years, they used to light another fresh set, and let them burn on the next few nights. We used never put the Christmas candles into candle sticks, as they were too

big, instead, we used to pack them into jam jars, and put in sand, earth or clay to keep them in position. We used to cover them with fancy paper, and we used always stick a few short bits of holly at the top of the jam jar. In the country, people used to cut a small round hole in a big turnip, and they used to soften the wax on the end of the candle into the turnip, and stick bits of holly and laurel leaves all around it. (NFC 1391: 128–9; Mrs Walshe, Kilrush, County Clare. Collector: Seán McGrath, January 1955.)

In Mrs McCarthy's house it was her husband who lit the candles:

If he wasn't in in time, that's before dark, we'd light the lamps 'till he'd come in. I'd always like to sprinkle a drop of holy water around the house and bless ourselves when the 'big' candles would be lighted. When the man of the house will have the candles lighted we must give him a dropeen.[6] (NFC 462: 232; Mrs McCarthy (62) Enniskean, County Cork. Collector: Diarmuid Ó Cruadhlaoich, January 1938.)

Bríghid Ní Ruairc, also from County Cork, gives the following account of the custom:

Candles are still lighted in all houses and in every window in the house on the nights of December 24th, 25th and 31st, and also on January 1st, 5th, and 6th. A few people light them on the night of December 26th. Even during the recent scarcity of candles this custom has been observed.[7] No homemade candles now. In pre-war years coloured Christmas candles, red or green were used but white was the usual colour. On Christmas morning when people are up early for mass they light some of the candles and leave them lighting till dawn. A Christmas candle should not be used for light on its own and nothing should be lighted off it – a paper, splinter or other candles. (NFC 1087: 161–2; Bríghid Ní Ruairc (70), Bantry, County Cork. Collector: Conchubhair Ó Ruairc, 1945.)

The following was written by Eibhlín Ní Mhurchadha, aged just 16, from west Kerry, in 1932:

Lastar coinnle ar gach fuinneog. Is gnáthach gurb í an mháthair a dheineann so. Má bhíonn an mháthair caillte deineann an leanbh is óige sa tigh é. Creidtear go mbíonn togha le fáil ag an té a lasann an choinneal. Má mhúchann an choinneal agus go mbíonn ort a lasadh athuair, comhartha é seo go mbeidh drochrath orthu i rith na bliana. Fágtar an choinneal ar lasadh go maidin sa chistin in onóir na Maighdine Muire agus mar chuimhneamh ar an oíche Nollag a bhí sí lasmuigh fadó nuair a rugadh an leanbh Íosa.

[Candles are lit in every window and it is usually the mother who lights them. If she is deceased the youngest child does it. It is believed that good things await the person who lights the candle. If the candle goes out, and

you have to light it again, this is a sign of misfortune for the coming year. The candle is left lit until morning in honour of the Virgin Mary and in remembrance of her being outdoors on the night the baby Jesus was born.] (NFC 22: 448; written by Eibhlín Ní Mhurchadha (16), Ballydavid, County Kerry, August 1932.)

In Donegal a blessed candle would be lit that hadn't been used up to then. In Bríd Ní Aghartaigh's house the rosary followed the supper, and then, once the house was tidied and people ready for bed, this candle would be lit:

Ag leath am luí nó mar sin bhíodh féasta mór ag teaghlach, ba chuma bocht nó saibhir iad. Nuair a bheadh achan nduine sáthach, déarfá cúig deichniúr déag. Ansin nuair a bheadh an teach sciobtha scuabtha sula rachadh an duine deireanach ina luí lasfaí coinneal choisricthe nár lasadh a roimhe, ceann úr mar a déarfá. D'fhágfaí an choinneal lasta ar thábla na cisteanaí os coinne na fuinneoige, agus mura mbeadh sé dóite ar maidin ní chuirfí as é go mbeadh sé caite. Teach ar bith a ghníodh seo chreid siad go raibh siad faoi choimirce na Maighdine Muire ar feadh an bliana úire. Ba le fáilte don Mhaighdean Mhuire an bhrí a bhí le dó na gcoinneal. Tá a fhios ag gach uile dhuine gurb é cothrom an oíche sin, fad, fad ó shoin a shiúil an Mhaighdean Bheannaithe go Bethlehem agus nach leigfeadh teach ar bith isteach í go dteachaigh sí ina stábla i mBethlehem. Is i gcuimhne bhrónach ar an aistear crua seo a lastar an choinneal agus le taispeáint don Mhaighdean

Mhuire dá mbeadh sí anois ar talamh agus í go hantráthach ar a cois ar an siúil a raibh sí ar na céadtaí agus na céadtaí bliain ó shoin, go mbeadh céad fáilte roimpi agus dídean a tí fhad agus ba thoil léi.

[As bedtime approached each household had a feast, whether they were rich or poor. Once everybody was well fed the rosary was said. Then, once the house was swept and tidied, and just before the last person went to bed, a blessed candle that hadn't been lit before would be set alight, a fresh one you might say. The candle would be left lighting on the kitchen table, above the window, and if it wasn't burnt out by morning it wouldn't be extinguished but left to burn itself out. Any house that did this was under the protection of the Virgin Mary for the new year. The candle was lit in order to welcome Mary. Everybody knows that on this night long ago, the Blessed Virgin walked to Bethlehem where no house would let her in until she came to a stable. It is in solemn memory of this cruel journey that the candle is lit, and to show the Virgin Mary, that if she were on earth now, walking in the dead of night as she was hundreds of years ago, that there would be a welcome for her, and a roof over her head.] (NFC 335: 136-8; Bríghid Ní Aghartaigh (30), Kilcar, County Donegal. Collector: Anna Ní Éigheartaigh, March 1936.)

As well as the Christmas candle, importance was given to the 'Yule log' or *'Bloc na Nollag,'* which was usually a block of bog deal. In some accounts it's mentioned as having

preventive powers against illness and accidents. The following is an account of the Christmas fire from Pádraig Ó hEideagáin:

> Long ago the head of the house brought in a huge stick of bog dale (deal), generally known as a black stick. He placed this across the whole hearth and got the coals towards the centre of it. This big stick was called then the 'Yule log.' The coals in the centre burned across the stick dividing it into two parts. One of these burned out on Christmas Eve and the second part was kept for Christmas Night (25th). It was not known that it had any curative powers, or even its ashes, in this area. The second part burned out completely on the 25th. (NFC 1084: 517; Pádraig Ó hEideagáin (54), Cooraclare, County Clare. Collector: Maighréad Bean Uí Mharthain, January 1945.)

Liam Neannáil recounts the following: *'Bhíodh teine mhór ins gach tigh Oíche Nollag. Bhíodh bloc mór adhmaid acu – 'Bloc na Nollag' do thugaidís air. Ní bhíodh aon adhmad speisialta ann. Do dhótaí é go léir* [There used to be a large fire in every house on Christmas Night. It was a large timber block – it was known as the 'Christmas block.' No particular type of wood was used. It used to be completely burnt out].' (NFC 1085: 16; Liam Neannáil (70), Grange, County Waterford. Collector: Risteàrd Neannáil, December 1944.)

Eamon Mac Tomáis from west Limerick said:

The 'Yule log' was placed upon the hearth Christmas Eve and a portion of the burned out cinder was preserved until St. Patrick's Day when it was rubbed in the form of a cross on the arms of the people, to keep away accidents. (NFC 1084: 105; Éamon Mac Tomáis (68), Moroe, County Limerick, Collector: Pádraig de Barra, December 1944.)

The following is from Labhrás Ó Cadhla of Cappoquin, County Waterford. In this area the block wasn't added to the fire until Christmas Day. The salmon fishing referred to was on the River Blackwater, which flows next to the town:

Bhíodh tine speisialta ag na daoine Oíche Nollag. Bloc giúise a bhíodh bainte ar feadh bliana nó mar sin. Chuirtí sa tine é timpeall a ceathair a' chlog tráthnóna Lae Nollag, agus an méid de ná beadh dóite ar maidin chuirtí amach é chun sliseoga a dhéanamh de. Bhídís san ag lucht iascach bhrádáin mar sholas nuair a bhídís ag iascach thar dlí i Mí na Féile Bríde.

[People always had a special fire on Christmas Night. A block of bog deal that had been cut for around a year was put into the fire around four in the afternoon on Christmas Day. Whatever was not burned the next morning was made into strips, and these strips were used by salmon fishermen for lights when they went out poaching in February.] (NFC 1084: 29; written by Labhrás Ó Cadhla (56), Cappoquin, County Waterford, February 1945.)

CHRISTMAS EVE

As mentioned, the lighting of the candle commemorates the plight of Mary and Joseph as they wander through Bethlehem in search of shelter. This story informs other customs such as leaving the doors open to welcome the Holy Family, or any stranger who finds themselves in such a predicament on Christmas Eve. Niall Ó Dubhthaigh tells us:

> *Bhí intinn ag na seandaoine nach raibh déirce ar bith a ba mhó a rachadh chun socair dá n-anam nó an déirce a bhéarfadh siad uatha in onóir ár Slánaitheoir troscadh Oíche Nollag Mór, agus siúd nach raibh mórán de mhaoin an tsaoil acu, rannfadh siad an ghreim a bheadh le cur ina mbéal leis an té a bheadh ag dul thart ag cruinniú na déirce.*
>
> [The old people believed that no act of charity was more beneficial to the soul than an act of charity on Christmas Eve in honour of our Saviour. Those less well-off would share the morsel going into their mouths with any beggar that came their way.] (NFC 932: 411; Niall Ó Dubhthaigh (69) (with help from his sister Eibhlín), Cloghaneely, County Donegal. Collector: Seán Ó hEochaidh, 1943.)

Willie Walsh of Kilrush describes the custom as follows:

> Doors should be always left on the latch, as they used to say the Holy Family might be wandering around looking for a place, not that they would come in, but the old people used to say that they used to find out how many

open doors would be waiting for them should they require shelter again. Women long ago used to leave a glass of wine and a slice of cake on the kitchen table for St. Joseph in case he would be hungry or tired on his travels, looking for a place to stay. Children think it is on account of Santa Claus that this be done. Most houses long ago took out the ashes from the hearth between six and nine p.m. on Christmas Night, and before going to bed they used to have the fire banked up so as to give warmth to any stranger who may enter, and also to have continuous fire all during Christmas. (NFC 1391: 130; Willie Walshe, Kilrush, County Clare. Collector: Seán McGrath, January 1955.)

The following tale from Dónal de Grás, of Glennamaddy, describes the charitable act of a man from his own area many years earlier:

An old man who lived near my house many years ago is said to have been sent to a blessed well for water for the Christmas supper on Christmas Eve at about 11pm. On reaching the well he is said to have seen a husband, wife and four children sitting on the brink of the well, perished with the hunger and cold. They asked him if he would give them a supper and a place to sleep until morning. He brought them to his house, shared his supper with them, and gave them a place to sleep. From that on he had plenty to eat and drink and was always very comfortable and

happy. He died a few years ago and the well in question is said to have closed up the night he died. The site of the well is still pointed out in a vale covered with weeds and grasses. (NFC 1089: 107–8; written by Dónal de Grás, Glennamaddy, County Galway, March 1945.)

Labhrás Ó Cadhla recounts how old people would sit up all night on Christmas Eve and leave water on the table which would turn to wine at midnight. In general, this belief is more commonly associated with the nights of New Year's Eve and 5 January:

Tugtar Oíche Nollag ar an oíche roimh an fhéile, agus ba ghnáth le seandaoine an oíche go léir do thabhairt suas gan luí ar leabain. Bhíodh dabhach mhór uisce istigh ann mar deirtí go ndéanfaí fíon den uisce ar uair an Mheán Oíche. D'ólaidís go leor den uisce agus chuirtí i gcoimeád i mbuidéal í ar feadh na bliana chun braon dó do thabhairt do dhuine nó do bheithíoch a mbeadh aon ghalar nó aicíd orthu.

[The night before the festival was known as Christmas Night and it was usual for the old people to stay up all night. A large tub of water was brought in and it used to be said that the water turned to wine at midnight. They used to drink a good bit of it and then keep it in a bottle for the year and give a drop to any person or animal that became sick.] (NFC 1084: 25; written by Labhrás Ó Cadhla, Cappoquin, County Waterford, February 1945.)

Tomás Ó Murchadh from west Limerick tells of the dead returning to their homes on Christmas Eve:

> Another custom of Christmas was the belief that the person who died during the year revisited the old home, and before the woman of the house retired for the night she prepared the table – bread and butter on a plate and a cup of tea, coloured and sweetened, and in some instances left a stimulant where 'twas known the deceased had a like for same. There's a yarn that in one instance the woman left a full bottle of whiskey for the deceased here and that in the morning the bottle was broken since she hadn't the foresight to uncork it. (NFC 1084: 149; Tomás Ó Murchadh (68), Abbeyfeale, County Limerick. Collector: Dáibhí Ó Consaidain, March 1945.)

For many, Christmas Eve was a night spent exclusively with family, with nobody expected to leave the house. In other areas, people called to their neighbours to wish them a Happy Christmas, and where Midnight Mass was celebrated, people would attend. Midnight Mass was rare in isolated rural areas. In the accounts of Midnight Mass the problem of drunken worshippers is a common theme:

> We never had Midnight Mass here until they had the one for the Holy Year in 1950 and again for the closing of it, but when they opened the church below over 109 years

ago now, they used to have Midnight Mass there on Christmas Night, but after three or four years they had to stop it as there was too many drunks going into the house of God, and one of the priests at the time, a Father Malachy Sweeney, cleared five or six of them from the church as they was drunk and they insulted him. (NFC 1391: 132; Tadhg Kelly, Kilrush, County Clare. Collector: Seán McGrath, January 1955.)

The following account from Mrs Patrick Murphy of Clonduff, County Down, has a slightly wry perspective on the Midnight Mass:

The blackout[8] almost put a stop to Midnight Mass. It was frowned upon by the bishops anyhow on account of the number of tipsy worshippers who turned up to pray – I mean to sleep, perchance to dream – aloud! But now that the blackout is relaxed, a number of enterprising priests have revived the Midnight Mass with the result that scores of people from the neighbouring parishes flocked to it, bringing their half-crowns with them. So now it is a question of restoring the Midnight Mass or taking up the Christmas collection on the Sunday before Christmas. Already both methods have been tried and I am inclined to think the odds are in favour of the Midnight Mass; the lights, the music, the crib, the sermon, and the general good humour associated with Christmas seem to induce people to a speculative half-crown, who never paid to a collection before. (NFC 1087: 33; Mrs Patrick Murphy (71), Clonduff, County Down. Collector: Francis McPolin, January 1945.)

Though people feared the fairies throughout the year, this fear intensified at certain times of the year, such as on May Eve. However, the fairies seem largely absent from the festival of Christmas. Malign presences such as the *Púca*,[9] or the Devil, who were known to appear to people on desolate roads or paths at night, are rarely mentioned either. The following, however, is a short tale from Donegal, set on a dark road, late on Christmas Eve, told by Niall Ó Domhnaill from Dunglow:

Fear a bhí ag gabháil an bealach mór go hantráthach Oíche Nollag amháin nuair a bhuail diúlach coimhthíoch leis agus ba ghairid gur thoisigh sé ag cur cruaidh air. Tháinig eagla ar an fhear nó d'aithin sé go maith nach dea-rud ar bith a bhí sa duine a bhí ag coinneáil coiscéim leis. Leis sin, rinne coileach scairt, phreab an fear dubh agus dúirt: 'Caithfidh mise imeacht, níl cead agam bheith ar mo chois i ndiaidh scairt an choiligh.' D'imigh sé mar bheadh splancadh neimhe ins an spéir agus ba ansin a d'aithin an fear gurbh é an Diabhal a bhí ann. Deir siad nach cóir do dhuine uaigneas a bheith air nuair a bhíos an coileach ag scairtí.

[Late on Christmas Eve a man was walking the road when a stranger began to gain on him. The man became afraid and knew that it wasn't anything good on his heels.

With that the cock crew; the devil man was startled and said: 'I must leave, I'm not permitted to be on foot after the cock crows'. He disappeared like a flash of lightning in the sky and it was only at that moment the man realised it was the Devil who stood before him. They say that a person shouldn't feel loneliness when the cock crows]. NFC 1143: 40; Niall Ó Domhnaill, Dunglow, County Donegal. Collector: Niall Mac Suibhne, January 1944.)

The notion of the cock warding off evil is an interesting one and had been investigated further by the Irish Folklore Commission. In 1943, the Commission asked its correspondents to seek information about the cock, following a letter from Professor J.J. Hogan of UCD, in which he sought to establish: 'if the following tradition as shown in Shakespeare (but not found now in English folklore) can be found in Ireland'. In the letter, he describes Shakespeare's reference to this tradition in *Hamlet*:

In Shakespeare's Hamlet I (157-164) Marcellus says of the ghost which has disappeared:

'It faded on the crowing of the cock.
Some say that ever 'gainst that season comes, wherein our Saviour's birth is celebrated.
This bird of dawning singeth all night long.
And, then they say no spirit dare stir abroad.
The nights are wholesome, then no planets strike,

No fairy tales, nor witch had power to charm.
So hallowed, and so gracious is that time.'

It appears from this passage that it was believed in Shakespeare's day (i) that for some nights immediately before Christmas the cock crows or sings all night (ii) that this averts all evil influences. No such beliefs survive in the folklore of England, and this passage is the only evidence that they ever did exist.[10] (NFC 1143: 2; extract from 'Seanchas Nollag' issued by The Irish Folklore Commission to its correspondents in 1943.)

In her essay on the many beliefs associated with Christmas Eve, Ríonach Uí Ógáin tells us that the cock's power in warding off evil can be traced back to pre-Christian times and was later assimilated into Christian tradition.[11] She refers to an international ballad called 'St Stephen and Herod' in which the saint tells Herod of the birth of Jesus. Herod says he will not believe it until the dead cock in front of him moves his wings and crows, which he duly does. In the English tradition, the cock was believed to utter the Latin words: '*Christus natus est*' (Christ is born). The following belief, not restricted to Christmastime, from Bantry, County Cork, is described by Conchubhar Ó Ruairc:

It was a general belief that the cock when crowing at night, for example from 9pm – 3am drove away all fairies and

púcaí. The fact that he did crow during those hours was sufficient proof that fairies were out and people usually got afraid, if he did crow, and made the sign of the cross or said: *'Go gcoiscrigh Dia sinn agus a choilichín'* [May God bless us and his small rooster]. (NFC 1143: 17; written by Conchubhair Ó Ruairc, Bantry, County Cork, September 1944.)

The following from Seán Ó Dúda in Ballydavid, County Kerry, tells of the people expecting to hear the cock crow at night in the run up to Christmas:

Tá sé comhairthe riamh go mbíonn na coiligh ag glaoch i dtosach oíche seachtain nó coicíos roimh Nollaig. Deirtear gur le háthas a bhíonn siad agus ag cur fáilte roimh Nollaig nó ag fógairt na Nollag a bheith ag teacht.

[The cocks were expected to crow at nightfall from about a week or a fortnight before Christmas. It is said that this display of joy was to announce and welcome the coming of Christmas.] (NFC 1143: 16; written by Seán Ó Dúda, Ballydavid, County Kerry, 1943.)

Interestingly, Niall Ó Dubhthaigh mentions the cock crowing in the run up to Christmas, both at night and during the day. However, he attributes their crowing to their fear of ending up on the dinner table. A cock crowing at night during the rest of the year foretold a death in the family, but at Christmas no superstitious significance was attached.

*Ní raibh meas ar chineál ar bith feola eile Lá Nollag ach feoil
éanlaithe – mhairbhfí coileach nó cearc agus sin an t-am
a mbíodh an eagla ar na coiligh bhochta. Ní bhainfeadh
suaimhneas ar bith oíche nó lá ar feadh seachtaine nó níos mó
roimh an Nollaig. Bheadh siad ag scairtí i lár na hoíche. Bheifí
ag dúil le bás duine sa teaghlach ach cha chuirfí suim ar bith i
scairteach na Nollag.*

[The only type of meat that was acceptable on
Christmas Day was fowl; a cock or hen would be killed and
the fear would take hold of the poor cocks. They wouldn't
settle day or night for a week or more before Christmas.
They'd crow in the middle of the night. A death in the
household would be expected normally, but no heed was
given to crowing at Christmas.] (NFC 932: 397; Niall Ó
Dubhthaigh, Cloghanneely, County Donegal. Collector:
Seán Ó hEochaidh, 1943.)

When the cock crew at midnight on Christmas Eve, it
was believed he was announcing the Saviour's birth: *'Níor
chuala ach amháin go nglaonn an coileach ag uair an mheon-
oíche: "Mac na hÓighe slán agus a namhaid ar lár."'* [All I've
ever heard is that the cock crows at the hour of midnight:
"The Son of the Virgin is safe and his enemies fallen."]

The farm animals were given a certain prominence on
Christmas Eve due to the fact they were present in the
stable and watched over the Baby Jesus after his birth. It
was widely believed that animals went on their knees at
midnight in honour of the Child's birth. The outhouses were

cleaned and decorated for Christmas. Animals also enjoyed extra food at Christmas. Tomás Mac Domhnaill tells us:

> Lamps left lighting in outhouses where cows were; to repay for company they afforded the Holy Family the first Christmas morning. All animals said to go to sleep on the night of 24th, except the serpent. In some parts the horse was excluded from receiving extra food due to his association with the Jewish people. (NFC 1084: 84; written by Tomás mac Domhnaill, Cloughjordan, County Tipperary, February 1945.)

Labhrás Ó Cadhla writes:

Thugtaí bia faoi leith do gach ainmhí ach amháin don chapall,
mar nuair a bhíonn gach ainmhí eile ag éirí ó bheith ina luí
téann siad ar a nglúinibh, ach amháin an capall; éiríonn sé
sin na cosa tosaigh ar dtúis. Adhrann gach ainmhí Dia ach
amháin an capall, mar deiridís gur ós na Giúdaigh a tháinig
sé ar dtúis.

[All of the animals got extra food except the horse,
because when the others arise after being asleep, they go
onto their knees first. However, the horse gets up with
his front legs first. Every animal worships God except the
horse, as it was said the horse originated from the Jewish
people.] (NFC 1084: 28; written by Labhrás Ó Cadhla,
Cappoquin, County Waterford, February 1945.)

It was firmly prohibited to go and observe the
phenomenon of the animals kneeling at midnight, and
anybody foolish enough to give into their curiosity
could expect punishment. The following is a cautionary
tale, one with added credence, since the teller, Niall Ó
Dubhthaigh, says he could name the protagonist but
refrains from doing so because the man's family were still
living nearby:

Tá sé aithriste ariamh insan cheantar seo go dtéid an t-asal síos
ar a ghlúine ar uair an mheon-oíche. Bhí fear agus dúirt sé go
bhfaigheadh seisean amach cé acu a bhí sin fíor nó nach raibh.
Nuair a tháinig an t-am don asal a dhéanamh, d'umhlaigh

sí síos ar a dá chois tosaigh, agus chonaic seisean go raibh an
ceart ag na seandaoine. Thug sé iarraidh an bóitheach a fhágáil
ansin, agus nuair a thug sé iarraidh na cosa a chur faoi ní raibh
cos aige le seasamh uirthi. Shiúil sé amach ar a lámha agus
ar a chosa, agus ón lá sin go dtí an lá a chuaigh sé i dtalamh
níor chuir sé an chos faoi. Chuala mé na seandaoine ag inse an
scéil sin céad uair in m'óige. Thiocfadh liom ainm an fhir sin a
thabhairt fosta ach tá barraíocht dá mhuintir beo thuas ansin
go fóill. Fuair sé an buile a thuill sé go maith, go ndéana Dia
trócaire air.

[It was always said around these parts that the donkey
goes on his knees at midnight. There was once a man
who decided he'd find out whether there was any truth in
it. When the time came for the donkey to kneel, she did
just that, and the man saw that the old people were right.
He went to stand up and leave the shed, but he couldn't
stand up. He crawled out, and from that day until the
day he died he never walked again. I must have heard
that tale a hundred times from the old people when I was
young. I could give you the man's name, but too many of
his people are still alive and living in the area. He got what
he deserved, may God have mercy on him.] (NFC 932:
411-3; Niall Ó Dubhthaigh (69), with help from his sister
Eibhlìn, Cloghaneely, County Donegal. Collector: Seán Ó
hEochaidh, 1943.)

Pádraic Ó Díscín recalls hearing about his uncle's curiosity
at midnight one Christmas Eve, when he decided to go
and see the animals kneeling:

An uncle told me that he went to try this on Christmas Night at the hour of twelve, but being frightened by something or other, and being only a lad, he ran for dear life, thinking it was the devil trying to frighten people away. (NFC 1089: 66-7; written by Pádraig Ó Díscín, Tuam, County Galway, 1944.)

The following poem was collected by Pádraig de Barra from a Mrs Guiney. It is certainly a rarity in that it places St Bridget within the Christmas tradition and names her as the first foster mother of Jesus. This is the only piece of Christmas lore I have found in which she is mentioned.[12]

Bríd the Fair was stole away
From Erin where she was born,
And now dwelling in Bethlehem so young
And so forlorn.
'Twas she who sighed for her parents dear
When far from her home and kin
She sadly toiled for a scanty dole,
A serving maid at the inn.
Bríd the Fair was first of all
The Holy Child to see,
Enthroned like a thing of Love,
Upon his mother's knee.
Where now the lantern star had shone,
In shafts of silver fire,

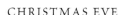

Bríd the Fair at Mary's feet
Who sooths the infant's cry
And held him in her gentle arms,
And crooned this lullaby.
This is the reason Bríd the Fair is everywhere adored,
And was the little foster mother of Our Lord.

(NFC 1084: 118; Mrs Guiney, Moroe, County Limerick.
Collector: Pádraig de Barra, December 1944.)

Though the exchange of gifts was not as big a part of Christmas as it is today, it was customary for neighbours to give each other presents of food or drink. It was also common for the better off to assist their neighbours who were not in a position to have a big Christmas dinner. Liam Neannáil from Waterford tells us:

Thugadh na comharsain bronntanais dá chéile; roimh an Nollaig ba ghnách iad a thabhairt. Eallaigh is mó a bhíodh á dtabhairt acu, gé nó turcaí, sicíní ramhra, píosa feola (bagún ar an mbairille) do dhaoine ná bíodh sé acu.

[The neighbours used to exchange presents, which were normally distributed before Christmas. Cattle, a goose or turkey, fattened chickens, or portions of meat (bacon on the barrel) were given to those who needed it. (NFC 1084: 18; Liam Neannáil (70), Grange, County Waterford. Collector: Risteárd Neannáil, December 1944.)

Bríghid Ní Ruairc provides a similar account:

> We always went out on Christmas Eve with presents of
> potatoes, milk and butter to the poor people. We took a
> quart of milk, lots of butter and a few stone of potatoes to
> each family. For two or three weeks before Christmas my
> mother used be gathering a churn to divide it on the poor.
> We used all get a ribbon or some new garment of clothes for
> Christmas. (NFC 1084: 162; Bríghid Ní Ruairc (70), Bantry,
> County Cork. Collector: Conchubhair Ó Ruairc, 1944.)

Mrs McCarthy speaks about gifts and giving at Christmas
time, and again we find that kindness towards neighbours
is of great import:

> But faith we can't forget the neighbours too. You know the
> ould people used to say: your best friend is your neighbour.
> An 'tis true too, for when anything is wrong 'tis for our
> neighbour we must run. So we can't forget 'thout[13] to give
> 'em some little bit; a bit o' butter, a jug o' milk or a gallon
> o' buttermilk for their baking, a bit o' bacon or something
> in that line. Poor people can't have much, as poor as wan[14]
> would be, you'd find some wan poorer an' we'll try an' give
> what we can afford; 'tis always done at Christmas time.
> (NFC 462: 233-4; Mrs Mccarthy (62), Enniskean, County
> Cork. Collector: Diarmuid Ó Cruadhlaoich, January
> 1938.)

CHRISTMAS EVE

Many people looked forward to gifts from relations abroad, especially from America. As mentioned earlier, the tradition of Santa Claus only begins to take root towards the end of the nineteenth century, with his fame spreading on an east to west trajectory. Tadhg Kelly speaks about Christmas presents in his youth:

> We used to get presents from my aunts in America, but then we used to get a 'butt of spuds'[15] from a few friends of the fathers, and we'd get at least three or four goose. You wouldn't get no goose now from a countryman, except from a very decent one. We used as youngsters hang up our stockings near the fireplace when we were going to bed, and we got little toys and presents but 'twas nearly all fruit like apples or oranges we used to get long ago. (NFC 1391: 132-3; Tadhg Kelly, Kilrush, County Clare. Collector: Seán McGrath, January 1955.)

It is clear from the following that Santa Claus had not reached north-west Donegal during Niall Ó Dubhthaigh's childhood in the 1880s:

> *Ní raibh iomrá ar Santa Claus nuair a bhí mise i mo thachrán ar chor ar bith. Níor chuala mé mo mháthair nó duine ar bith den tseanmhuintir ag trácht go raibh iomrá ar bith ar a leithéid ar chor ar bith ina n-óige san ach oiread. Bhí sé ina ghnás acu bronntanais bheaga a thabhairt dá chéile; péire stocaí nó miotógaí, nó ball éadaigh de shórt inteacht mar sin. Bhí sé ina*

ghnás mór fosta haincearsain dheasa shíoda a bheith ag dul san am sin, agus b'fhéidir go gceannódh cailín ceann deas acu sin don bhuachaill a raibh sí mór leis. Tá cuimhne mhaith agam tá tuairim ar dheich mbliana fiche ó shoin, bhí máistir agus máistreás scoile istigh ar oileán Inis Bó Finne anseo, agus nuair a bheadh an mháthair ag smachtú na bpaistí nó b'fhéidir ag iarraidh orthu gnóthaí beaga inteacht a dhéanamh, déarfadh an mháthair leo mura ndéanfadh siad an rud a d'iarrfadh sí orthu, agus iad a bheith maith nach dtiocfadh Santa Claus anuas an simléar le rud ar bith a chur ina gcuid stocaí nuair a thiocfadh an Nollaig. Bhí mná aosta ar an oileán ins an am sin, agus go leor acu nár fhág an t-oileán ariamh agus nach raibh focal Béarla acu agus níor chuala siadsan ariamh trácht ar an fhear uasal seo gur chuala siad máistreás na scoile ag caint air.

[There was no mention of Santa Claus when I was a young fella. I never heard my mother or any of the old people speak of him. It was customary to exchange gifts; a pair of stockings or gloves, or some item of clothing. Silk handkerchiefs were popular at the time and maybe a girl might buy one for a boy she was friendly with. I can remember about 30 years ago there was a school master and school mistress on Inisbofin,[16] and when the mother was disciplining her children, or asking them to do bits around the house, she'd say to them that if they weren't good, Santa Claus wouldn't come down the chimney to put anything in their stockings. The old women on the Island at the time, many of whom had never left it, nor had they a word of English, well, they had never heard

of this fine noble man until the school mistress spoke of him.] (NFC 932: 448-9; Niall Ó Dubhthaigh (69) with help from his sister Eibhlín, Cloghaneely, County Donegal. Collector: Seán Ó hEochaidh, 1943.)

Pádraic Ó hAichir writes from the Aran Islands:

Insan seanaimsir, ní raibh daoine chomh tugtha do bhronntanais bheaga a thabhairt ach thugtaí bainne, im, searc, bagún nó rud ar bith mar sin do dhaoine bochta nach mbeadh mórán acu. Le suim blianta tugtar bronntanais do leanaí i bhfoirm Santa Claus; tá sé sin coitianta le cúpla scór bliain. Ach, ba ghnách le chuile dhuine airgead a fháil ón a gclann in America faoi Nollaig.

[In the old days, people weren't so preoccupied with giving each other presents, but poor people used to receive milk, butter, shark, bacon and the like. For a number of years now children receive presents in the form of Santa Claus; something that's been common for the last forty years. It was usual for everybody to get money from their family in America during Christmas.] (NFC 1089: 12; written by Pádraic Ó hAichir, Kilronan, Aran, County Galway, March 1945.)

In Tuam, County Galway Pádraic Ó Díscín remembers the absence of Santa Claus from his childhood in the 1880s and his eventual arrival from America:

AN IRISH CHRISTMAS

In my early days, to my own knowledge, few gifts were given to children. Santa Claus was not even mentioned and I was a bit mystified when I heard Yanks returned making much of Santa Claus. In this locality the Santa Claus notion was introduced by Yankee-Land customs. Now Santa Claus holds the fort all by himself, too much is made of him. (NFC 1089: 66; written by Pádraic Ó Díscín, Tuam, County Galway, December 1944.)

THREE

Christmas Day

Christmas Day, in Irish *Lá Nollag,* is also known as Big Christmas (*Nollaig Mhór* or *Lá Nollag Móire*) or the Men's Christmas (*Nollaig na bhFear*). Amhlaoibh Ó Loingsigh in Coolea, County Cork believed it was called the Big Christmas because it was the day when people enjoyed the biggest meal of the year, and he has the following explanation for calling it the Men's Christmas:

Measaim gurb é seo mar a bhfuair an Nollaig Mhór an t-ainm Nollaig na bhFear, mar ba ghnáth go mbeadh fear as gach aon tigh amuigh lá nó dhó roimhré ag soláthar neithe ina comhair agus dá mbeadh aon ní in easnamh b'iad na fir a gheibheadh milleán ina thaobh.

[I think this is why the Big Christmas got the name the Men's Christmas: A man from each house was usually out gathering supplies for a day or two beforehand, and if anything was lacking then it was the men who used to get the blame.] (NFC 1084: 217; Amhlaoibh Ó Loingsigh

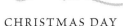

CHRISTMAS DAY

(72), Coolea, County Cork. Collector: Cáit Uí Liatháin, December 1944.)

The day would begin with attendance at an early Mass. It was believed that the first Mass on Christmas Day morning was worth twenty in terms of receiving indulgences from God. It was known as *Aifreann na Gine* (The Nativity Mass). There was a saying that went: '*Aifreann na Gine, Aifreann is Fiche.*' ('The Navity Mass, Twenty Masses.') This particular morning Mass was traditionally held at a very early hour: '*Ins an seanaimsir bhíodh Aifreann an-mhoch Lá Nollag (Aifreann na Gine), tuairim a cúig a chlog ar maidin.*' [In the old days Christmas Day Mass used to be very early, at around 5 a.m.] (NFC 1089: 13; written by Pádraic Ó hAichir, Kilronan, Aran, County Galway, March 1945.)

People in isolated areas often had quite a journey to make in the dark. Mrs McCarthy describes her Christmas morning:

> Oh faith, we must try and get the cows milked and all the cattle fed in time to go to early Mass on Christmas morning. We'll have to be lavin'[1] here in the dark, faith, three miles in an old 'common car'.[2] (NFC 462: 231; Mrs McCarthy (62), Enniskean, County Cork. Collector: Diarmuid Ó Cruadhlaoich, January 1938.)

Isabel Grubb speaks of a strange encounter some people had on the way to Christmas morning Mass:

Pat O'Neill told me that about one hundred years ago some people from here, going to 6am Mass, saw a number of people crossing the road by a Mass path, and they told them they were the people buried in one old churchyard, Dysert, going to hear Mass at another, Templeonogh. (NFC 1084: 34; Mary O'Neil/Isabel Grubb, Seskin, County Tipperary, Collector: Isabel Grubb, 1944.)

Willie Moody in Kilrush, County Clare, recalls Christmas morning when he was a boy:

Everyone in the town and parish used to be nearly at the seven o'clock Mass on Christmas Morning, and it used to be dark when we would be going there. We used to wish one another a Happy Christmas, and then after Mass, when you came out, you'd meet all your pals and if you had anything new like a new breeches or a new jumper, they would be codding you as to was it Santa Claus that brought it to you. (NFC 1391: 134, Willie Moody, Kilrush, County Clare. Collector: Seán McGrath, January 1955.)

The following superstitions were collected by Pádraig de Barra in Moroe, County Limerick:

Old people long ago at Christmas always took a piece of the moss and a straw from the crib and put the two small parts in their purses, believing that by doing same, and keeping the moss and straw in their purses, they would never be

short of money. Holy water taken from the church on Christmas Day was also believed to have curative powers. holy water was kept for seven years and there was believed to be a cure in it. People who went to the church for holy water were warned by their parents not to give any of it to any person along the road. The head of the house should take the first sup[3] out of the bottle. (NFC 1084: 120-1; Written by Pádraig de Barra, Moroe, County Limerick, December 1944.)

Christmas Day Mass gave people a chance to exchange greetings with neighbours they hadn't seen up until then. Liam Neannáil in County Waterford recounts the following:

Tugadh na comharsain na gnáthbheannachtaí dá chéile an lá san díreach mar a dhéantar i mBéarla anois: 'Nollaig fé shéan agus fé mhaise dhuit,' nó 'go dtuga Dia Nollaig mhaith dhuit' agus an freagra a gheibhtí: 'go mba hamhlaidh dhuit agus mórán díobh.'

[The neighbours greeted each other in the usual way, just as is the case in English now: 'A very Happy Christmas to you,' or 'May God grant you a good Christmas,' and the usual reply was 'and many happy returns and may you have many more.'] (NFC 1084: 19-20; Liam Neannáil (70), Grange, County Waterford. Collector: Risteárd Neannáil, December 1944.)

Mrs Murphy of County Down reflects on Christmas Greetings:

As for the country folk: 'I wish you a Happy Christmas' seems to have changed in recent years into 'A Happy Christmas to you', and even that seems to be too much for many of them now. Of course the postman and people like that still continued to wish you a Merry Christmas, just as a gentle reminder to wake up your generosity. In general the men folk seem rather shy of wishing you a Happy Christmas. They generally leave it to you to take the initiative and then they manage to say 'the same to yourself' and sometimes they will add 'and many of them'. The women are much bolder in that respect. But both men and women appear to feel more at their ease in wishing a Happy New Year. I wonder is that due to Scottish influence, or to our natural shyness in mentioning things religious. But alas! all our old greetings are dying out. You could walk the length of the street now on a fair day with a brand new suit on you, and not one would say 'Health to Wear' O tempora o mores! (NFC 1087: 34; Mrs Patrick Murphy (71), Clonduff, County Down. Collector: Francis McPolin, January 1945.)

Pádraic Ó hAichir describes the Christmas greetings heard in Kilronan on Aran: *"Nollaig mhaith dhuit" agus an freagra "go mba hé dhuit" nó "mo chuid den Nollaig ort". Má théann duine isteach i dteach deirfidís: 'go dtuga Dia Nollaig*

mhaith dhíbh.' [On Christmas Day people used to say: 'Have a good Christmas,' and the answer was 'same to you.' If people went into a house they'd say: 'may God give you all a good Christmas']. (NFC 1089: 13; written by Pádraic Ó hAichir, Kilronan, Aran, County Galway, March 1945.)

People usually went to Mass fasting and then, once home, and having eaten breakfast, preparations began for the Christmas dinner. Amhlaoibh Ó Loingsigh gives the following account from Coolea, County Cork:

Bhíodh formhór na ndaoine ar céadlongadh an mhaidin so agus nuair a thiocfaí abhaile ón Aifreann is ea d'íosfaí bricfeast. Ansan do thosnódh dinnéar a chur i dtreo. Bheadh gé le róstadh nó le beiriú ins gach tigh, ba chuma saibhir nó bocht, mar bhíodh géanna fálta mar thabhartaisí ag an muintir ná bíodh géanna acu féin. Bheadh prátaí i gcomhair an dinnéir seo agus timpeall a cúig a'chlog um thráthnóna ab ea dheinidís an béile a chaitheamh. Ní raibh aon phaidir ag baint leis an mbéile sin ach amháin go ndeineadh gach duine iad féin a choisreacan le linn éirí ón mbord agus déarfaidís os ard: 'An Té thug an bheatha so dhúinn, go dtuga sé an bheatha shíoraí d'ár n-anam.' Do bheadh tae agus na soláistí eile acu gan mhoill tar éis dinnéir agus na neithe céanna timpeall a haon déag a' chlog istoíche.

[Most people fasted on Christmas morning, but when they came home from Mass they'd sit down for breakfast. After that, dinner was prepared. A goose was roasted or boiled in every house, whether rich or poor. Those who did not have geese themselves were given a gift of a goose.

Potatoes accompanied the meal, and it was around 5 o'clock when they sat down to eat. There was no special prayer, but everyone would bless themselves when they rose from the table and they'd say aloud: 'May the one who gave us life, give eternal life to our soul.' Shortly after the dinner they'd have tea and sweet things and have more of the same at around 11 o'clock.] (NFC 1084: 213; Amhlaoibh Ó Loingsigh (72), Coolea, County Cork. Collector: Cáit Uí Liatháin, January 1945.)

Tone O'Dea gives a picture of Christmas Day during his childhood at the end of the nineteenth century:

My father used always buy a big pig's head, and my mother would have boiled this the day before Christmas Eve, and we used all be at seven o'clock Mass on Christmas morning, and when we'd come in, we used have this pig's head for the breakfast. We used to have a goose stuffed with breadcrumbs and onions for our dinner, and we used to have a bit of home cured salty bacon with it. Then for the tea we used to have the 'leavings' of the dinner and the pig's head again, and then my mother used to cut slices off the pudding, and she used to fry them in dripping on the griddle, and that used to be the nicest of it all. One thing every house had at Christmas Day, and they usedn't have the same again for another year, was custard or jelly. Christmas Day was the one day in the year when a table cloth used to be laid on every table for all the meals, and about forty-five or fifty years ago the women started putting down 'skin plates', and a lot of the old people used to say that 'twas how the people now were full of queer notions. When we were grown up my three brothers and myself, we used to get one bottle of stout from my mother of Christmas night, and by grown up I mean I was thirty-two and my two brothers were only a few years younger than me. No one was supposed to leave their own homes on Christmas night, 'twas unheard of to go out of doors. This still persists today in many homes in this district. (NFC 1391: 126-7, Tone O'Dea, Kilrush, County Clare. Collector: Seán McGrath, January 1955.)

Tadhg Kelly, also from Kilrush, talks about the plum pudding:

Years and years ago they used to stick a bit of plain holly in the big plum pudding, and when my mother would be cutting bits for us, she was ever so careful, so that the bit of holly would not fall out or be touched by the knife. I often saw the biteen[4] of holly to stay until there was only a thin wisp of the big pudding left, and then this was burned too. (NFC 1391: 125; Tadhg Kelly, Kilrush, County Clare. Collector: Seán McGrath, January 1955.)

Staying in Kilrush, County Clare, Willie Moody gives an account of Christmas Day during his childhood. Interestingly, he mentions a common practice of going out hunting (what he calls 'croosting'[5]) the wren before Christmas dinner in preparation for St Stephen's Day. It is also noteworthy in his account that the pubs were open on Christmas Day. After Irish independence, with the introduction of the Intoxicating Liquor Act of 1927, pubs were prohibited from opening on Christmas Day. This changed the nature of the day in Ireland.[6] Though people did socialise during the day, the practice of not leaving the house on Christmas Day night is mentioned again here:

After our breakfast, we used to go out 'croostin' that day. That was out trying to kill a wren so as to hang him off the bush on the Wren's Day. We used to all need to be back for our dinner, and my father would lock the front door, and we'd all sit down in our places, and have it. The Christmas dinner was always lonely, especially if one from the house had been buried since the last Christmas, and if such was the case, we were supposed to say to ourselves: 'The Lord have mercy on the soul.' Then either my father or mother would say, just before we started: 'God grant that we may be all alive, together and here again, this time twelve months.' None of us would leave the table until he and my mother were finished and then we would have to ask him to leave. We used to play pitch-and-toss[7] at the Glin Cross that evening, or else we'd play 'quaiths'[8] with stones and corks. One year they had horse races and donkey races behind in Scuff Point strand, but there was a big row there, over who won the race, and the police wouldn't let them be held there anymore. The bigger fellows used to be hanging around the public houses listening to the men inside singing their eyes out. The pubs used to do a great trade then. We would have our tea at seven o'clock, but devil damn the one of us, would be let out afterwards. Not even my oldest brother, and he was nearly thirty then. My father used even go for the bucket of water himself on Christmas night, as he wouldn't let one of us stir outside the door at all. (NFC 1391: 134-5; Willie Moody, Kilrush, County Clare. Collector: Seán McGrath, January 1955.)

Dónal de Grás, from Glennamaddy, speaks of not leaving the house at all on Christmas Day and offers the following explanation, which I haven't seen mentioned in any of the sources I've consulted: 'Nobody leaves the house on that day as it is supposed Our Lord visits each house specially and separately.' (NFC 1089: 105; written by Dónal de Grás, Glennamaddy, County Galway, March 1945.)

Mrs McCarthy highlights her frugality when asked whether she ate a turkey or a goose on Christmas Day:

Faith and indeed I don't. 'Tis more I'd want the price of wan[9] for something else, a pair of boots, or the makings of a bawneen[10] for the man or something that way. A bit of bacon and a turnip will do us very well and sure 'tis thankful we ought to be to have it. A good currant cake and a slice of barn brack will go nice enough with a cup of tae.[11] (NFC 462: 223; Mrs McCarthy (62), Enniskean,

CHRISTMAS DAY

County Cork. Collector: Diarmuid Ó Cruadhlaoich,
January 1938.)

On the Aran Islands the following practice predates the
eating of goose or turkey at Christmas: '*Roimh an Nollaig
mharótaí mart (bó nó bullán), agus cheannódh chuile dhuine
a d'fhéadfadh píosa de le haghaidh Lá Nollag. Is le deireanas
a thosaigh na géabha agus na turcaithe ag éirí coitianta Lá
Nollag.*' [Before Christmas, a cow or a bullock was killed,
and everybody with the means would buy a portion for
Christmas Day. It is only in recent times that geese and
turkeys have become common on Christmas Day.] (NFC
1089: 13; written by Pàdraic Ó hAichir, Kilronan, Aran,
County Galway, March 1945.)

The large traditional hurling and football matches,
once held on Christmas Day, have now vanished. The
descriptions that follow outline how the games were
played before the standardised rules of the Gaelic Athletic
Association, first founded in 1884. Firstly, a description
from west Limerick of preparations for the Christmas Day
hurling match:

Long before the feast some enthusiast had prepared the
hurling ball of the period. A little tin or iron box or even a
large sea shell (and sometimes such an article as a rosary-
bead box stolen from the mother), containing a few grains
of shot, was wrapped around with woollen thread, bits
of cork and gutta-percha. The ball was then covered with

leather, carefully sewn. The ball was larger than that used in hurling today. And so hurling, abandoned for some time in the early winter, was renewed on Christmas Day. Boys and girls in their best suits flocked to the gaoling and the flying ball, struck by the *camán*,[12] gave a glorious sound much louder than that from the modern *sliotar*.[13] (NFC 1084: 97; written by Liam Danaher, Athea, County Limerick, 1944.)

In modern times the game of hurling is not associated with County Donegal. The following account of Christmas Day hurling in Donegal, by Niall Ó Dubhthaigh, describes a furious game of bruising physicality:

Chruinneodh na buachaillí óga thart ansin go dtí páirceanna réidh mura mbeadh an sneachta ró-dhomhain agus thoiseodh an iomáin acu agus mhaireadh an iomáin sin acu go dtéadh sé a dhubhsholas. Sin mar a chaitheadh siad Lá Nollag fosta. Ba ghnáthach leo dhá chineál iomána a dhéanamh fosta: iomáin ard agus iomáin thalamh. Bhí an iomáin ard ina cluiche iontach agus, in amanna, ina hiomáin gharbh. Rachadh fir dhá bhaile fad leis an chríoch eadar an dá bhaile. Bhéarfadh siad leo an seanduine ab aosta a thiocfadh leo a fháil fá na bailte agus bhéarfadh siad an chraig dósan le caitheamh suas. Chomh luath agus a chaithfeadh an seanduine an chraig in airde d'imeodh an tóir ina dhiaidh; fir bhaile amháin ag dréim lena thabhairt ar an taobh s'acu féin agus an dream eile ag iarraidh a choinneáil ar an taobh s' acu féin. Bhéarfadh an

taobh a ba láidre leo an chraig ansin, b'fhéidir míle talamh,
agus an mhuintir eile ina ndiaidh ag iarraidh a philleadh,
agus tá mise ag inse duit go mbíodh rása ansin. Bhí an iomáin
thalamh ceart go leor agus ní raibh leath oiread masla ar an
mhuintir a bhíodh ina gcionn. Sheasadh an dá fhoireann
os coinne a chéile ar an pháirc agus dhéanfadh foireann acu
a ndícheall báire a chur isteach ar an fhoireann eile, agus
b'fhéidir go gcaithfeadh siad rith an tráthnóna ag dul dó sin.
Bhíodh siad garbh go leor le chéile in amanna agus iomaí duine
acu a tharraing ar an bhaile tráthnóna agus cneamháin air.
Chonaic mé iad go minic ag dul amach go dtín a muineál ins
an abhainn i ndiaidh na craige, ag iarraidh a bheith ag baint
dá chéile agus is iomaí duine acu ar briseadh a méara agus a
lámha leis na camáin ins na laethaibh sin.

[The young lads would assemble on level fields if the
snow wasn't too deep and then the hurling would start,
and the game would go on until it was dark. This was
how Christmas Day was spent. There were two types of
hurling: hurling in the air and ground hurling. Hurling
in the air was a great game and at times a rough one.
Men from two towns would head towards the boundary
between the two places. They would get the oldest man
who could travel and give him the hard ball to throw in.
As soon as he threw the ball up, men from one side would
try to bring it to their side, while the other group tried to
keep it in their territory. The strongest team might take
the ball a mile and the other side would chase them trying
to retrieve it, and I'm telling you that was some race. The

ground hurling was alright and wasn't as strenuous on the people playing it. The two teams would face each other, with each side trying to score, and maybe they'd spend the entire afternoon at this. They were often rough and many a man came home wounded in the evening. I often saw them neck-deep in the river after the ball, and the hurleys broke a lot of fingers and hands in those days.] (NFC 932: 455-7; Niall Ó Dubhthaigh (69) with help from his sister Eibhlín, Cloghaneely, County Donegal. Collector: Seán Ó hEochaidh, 1943.)

Football, played over a wide terrain in a similar fashion, was also a feature of Christmas Day in many parts. The following is from west Kerry and is from an unpublished semi-fictional account of life in the west Kerry Gaeltacht by Mícheál Ó Sé. In his introduction he says the book is an account of the life of an Irish-speaking fisherman. While it is a realistic portrayal of life and of the language spoken in this area, he says all names are fictional and that names and events described do not refer to any person alive or dead.

Ní raibh aon chaitheamh aimsire ba mhó go gcuirtí suim ann an uair úd ná an cluiche peile a bhíodh idir an dá pharóiste – b'fhéidir nach ceart peil a thabhairt ar an gcluiche fé mar a dheintí é d'imirt an uair úd. Is mór an tslacht atá tagtha ar an gcluiche ó shoin. Ní raibh liathróid dheas, chruinn, chórach le fáil sa tsiopa an uair úd. Níorbh fholáir do dhuine

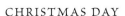

dea-lámhach éigin ceann a dhéanamh de sheithe asail agus de
lamhnán bó. D'fhéach Tadhg na Daibhche chuige ná beadh
aon easpa liathróide ar fhearaibh an pharóiste Lá Nollag.
Fuair sé seithe asail agus do leasaigh sé í i seanchorcán le
salann, agus le haol. Nuair a bhí sé leasaithe do ghearraigh sé
amach dhá phíosa chiorclacha agus pláta mar mhúnla aige.
D'fhuaigh sé suas le chéile an dá phíosa agus d'fhág sé poll
mar bhéal. D'iompaigh sé an taobh tuathail amach díobh
agus chuir sé lamhnán bó isteach tré pholl an bhéil. Bhí sé ag
séideadh gaoithe tré choinnlín isteach sa lamhnán nó go raibh
an liathróid chomh teann le hubh. Chuir sé ball bróige mar
bhéal-shreang ansan fé, agus d'fháisc sé suas é. Muna raibh an
liathróid sin cumtha, córach féin, ní bhfuair aoinne aon locht
mar ní raibh dul amach ar a mhalairt. Tar éis an dinnéir Lá
Nollag is ea do buaileadh amach an liathróid. Bhíodar ón dá
pharóiste ann, beag is mór, lag is láidir. Bhí seandaoine ann,
gurbh é a thug iad a bheith ag féachaint ar na himreoirí chun a
bheith á moladh nó á gcáineadh, do réir mar a bhí tuillte acu,
agus chun a bheith á gcur i gcomparáid leo féin nuair a bhíodar
óg. Bhí mná óga ann chun na himreoirí a spriogadh chun lútha
agus chun gaisce. Bhí leanaí beaga cosnochta ann agus iad
ag rith sall agus anall agus ag liúireach le mire agus meidhir
na hóige. Ní raibh aon chuimse le huimhir na n-imreoirí
ná aon teora le páirc na himeartha. Bhí gach aon fhear óg
acmhainneach sa pharóiste amuigh, ba chuma an raibh duine
ina choinnibh ag an bparóiste eile nó ná raibh. Níor deineadh
aon chomhaireamh, olc ná maith, ar na foirne, ná níor
chuimhnigh aoinne ar thabhairt fén a leithéid a dhéanamh,

agus tá sé tugtha fé ndeara ná raibh sé ariamh mar leithscéal ag an dtaobh do bhí cloíte gur lia a bhí an taobh eile. Bhí fairsinge an dá pharóiste mar pháirc imeartha, a sléibhte chomh maith lena mbánta. Ní raibh aon fhear cirt i láthair. Bhí cead saor ag gach aoinne lascadh a tharrac ar an liathróid pé treo gur maith leis é, pé uair a d'fhéadfadh sé é. Níor gá d'imirtheoir í a lascáil ar aon chor dá mba mhian leis é, ach í a bhualadh féna ascaill agus rith léithe faid a bheadh ina chroí agus fanacht ag rith léithe nó go dtabharfaí chun na talún é, de chóir nó de éagóir. Nuair ba de éagóir é, agus is amhlaidh ba ghnáthaí, ní raibh aoinne i mbun sásaimh a bhaint as an bhfear a dhein í. Bhí gach aoinne ar a chomhairle féin agus an fear ba threise in uachtar. Ní raibh féachaint do chlaí, ná do scairt, do dhíg ná do ghleann. Ba chuma cén áit go dtitfeadh an liathróid, bíodh sé fliuch nó tirim, bog nó cruaidh, bhíodh an scuaine sa mhullach uirthi agus gach aoinne ag réabadh is ag únfairt is ag raideadh. Ba mhinic a tugadh an liathróid tamall maith mar sin in aon bhall amháin, agus fiche nó daichead duine ag stracadh agus ag bearradh ar a chéile, ag iarraidh teacht uirthi. Mo thruasa an té go mbíodh sé de mhí-ádh air a bheith ceangailte ina lár istigh. Ní raibh fead ná adharc le séideadh mar chomhartha chun stad, ná aon chlár cuntais chun a thaispeáint cén taobh a bhí ag buachaint. Do thosnaíodh an cluiche ar an gclaí teorainn, agus bhí an bua le bheith ag an dream go mbeadh an liathróid ag a' baile acu ar thitim na hoíche.

[One of the most compelling pastimes at this time was the football match between the two parishes, though maybe it's not correct to call the game, as it was played at

the time, football. The game has advanced greatly since then. They didn't have nice neat round footballs in the shops back then. Somebody who was good with their hands would make one from the skin of a mule and a cow's bladder. Tadhg na Daibhche made sure there was no lack of balls for the men of the parish on Christmas Day. He took the skin of a mule and cured it in an old pot with salt and lime. Once it was cured he cut out two circular shapes using a plate as a mould. He sewed the two pieces together, leaving a hole as a mouth. He turned them inside out and he put the cow's bladder in through the hole. He inflated the ball through the hole until the ball was as firm as an egg. He used a piece of a shoe to string up the mouth, and then tightened it up. If the ball wasn't fully right, nobody ever found fault with it as they knew no better. The ball was let loose after dinner on Christmas Day. The two parishes were present, big and small, weak and strong. There were old people present, who came along to praise and condemn, as they deemed deserving, and to compare the players with themselves when they were young. Young women came along to encourage the men in their great feats. Young barefoot children were there, running around, shouting with the joy and delight of youth. There was no limit to the amount of players or to the size of the playing field. All the young and able men of the parish were out, whether they had someone to mark them from the other parish or not. The teams were never counted nor did it ever cross anybody's mind to do so. And it should

be noted that no losing team ever used it as an excuse that the opposing one had too many players. The expanse of the two parishes was the playing field, mountains as well as the plains. There was no referee present. A player could strike the ball in any direction he wanted, at any time he chose. A player didn't have to strike the ball at all; he could just put it under his arm and run with all his might until he was dragged to ground, fairly or unfairly. If it was unfair, as it usually was, there was no satisfaction to be garnered from the offender; everybody was out for themselves with the strongest man gaining the upper hand. There was no regard to a fence, or bush, dike or glen. It didn't matter where the ball fell, whether it was wet or dry, soft or hard, a crowd would be down on it, ripping and rolling. Sometimes the ball would stay in one spot with twenty or forty people pulling and dragging each other to get hold of it. Pity the man trapped in the middle of it. There was no whistle or horn to stop the game nor any record of the score to show who was winning. The game began at the boundary fence, and the winner was the team in possession of the ball at nightfall.] (NFC 1123, 176-9; written by Mícheál Ó Sé, Ballydavid, County Kerry.)

four

St Stephen's Day and the Day of the Holy Innocents

O n St Stephen's Day spirituality and religious observance is less evident, though for some it was a fast day when they abstained from meat. Much like today, many people left their homes after a quiet Christmas Day in search of recreation. In the country, outdoor pursuits such as fox hunting, coursing, and horse racing were popular. The tradition most associated with St Stephen's Day is the gathering of the Wren Boys and their journey from house to house to entertain and collect money. This tradition is still strong in many places today and has been revived in areas where it had died out. A key difference, however, is the fact that traditionally the Wren Boys brought a real dead wren on a bush or tree, which, as we have seen, was hunted on Christmas Day. It was believed that the wren betrayed Stephen to those hunting him when he flew from a bush in which Stephen was hiding. By the middle of the twentieth century the tradition had gone into decline, facing opposition from the clergy and the more respectable within the community, who were often appalled by some of the rowdiness and drinking associated with the Wren Boys. An example of this opposition can be found in Callan, County Kilkenny, as far back as 1828, in *The Diary of Amhlaoibh Ó Súilleabháin/Cín Lae Amhlaiobh*, where he writes on the 26 December: '*Grathain an bhaile ag imeacht ó dhoras go doras, le dreoilín i gcrann cuilinn, ag iarraidh airgid chum bheith ar meisce um dheireadh lae. Is olc an nós a thabhairt dóibh é.*' [The riff-raff of the town going from door to door, with a wren on a holly bush, gathering money in order to be drunk at the end of the day. It is a bad custom to give it to them.][1]

The following is a comprehensive account of St Stephen's Day from Ring, County Waterford:

Lá mór spóirt is fiaigh ba ea agus is ea Lá Féile Stiofáin. Ba mhian le daoine tuirse bídh na Nollag do chur díobh. Téann an foghlaeir ag foghlaeireacht mar tagann Lá le Stiofáin i lár an tséasúir chuige sin. Théadh agus téann go fóill ag fiach an mhadra rua. Bíonn cruinniú fé leith de chonairt con a leanann an madra rua. Is gnách go mbíonn an cruinniú san áit chéanna in aghaidh na bliana ar an lá sin agus óltar deochanna sara leogtar chun bóthair. Deirtear go mbíodh ráiseanna capall ag crosaire Chadhla san tseanaimsir ach is gnách go dtéann lucht leanúna an spóirt sin go dtí na ráiseanna oifigiúla i Luimneach agus in áiteanna eile an lá sin i láthair na linne seo. Gabhann buachaillí an dreoilín timpeall ó áit go háit an lá sin. Is minic a bhíonn cailíní i measc na scafairí. Fadó, is bia is deochanna a bhailídís agus b'fhéidir roinnt beag airgid a gheibhtí ag na tithe móra agus dheintí gach aon rud a roinnt ar na bochtaibh. Airgead a bhíonn uatha fé láthair agus roinntear an t-airgead sin ar na baill a bhíonn sa bhfoireann Dreoilín. Chaithidís an tsaghas seanbhalcaisí éadaí a bhíodh le fáil timpeall an tí, mar tá seanbhrístí, seanghúnaí, seanhataí, nó culaith fé leith déanta as cadás ildathach. Is minic bhídís seachtain ag cur i gcóir don ócáid sin. Is gnách go gcaitheadh gach duine aghaidh fidil. Go minic is aghaidh fidil ceannaithe a chaithfí ach uaireanta dhéanfaí aghaidh fidil de phíosa ceirte nó de chraiceann coinín nó de sheithe de shaghas éigin. Chuirfí ribíní agus ornáidí iolsaghasanna ar na hataí. Is iontach na pleidhcí de hataí a chaithtí. Is gnách go dtugadh gach buíon dreoilín tor cuilinn timpeall leo. Bhíodh ornáidí de ribíní ildathacha agus stiallacha de pháipéar daite in airde air. Bhíodh dreoilín in airde ar a bharra leis, istigh i lár an chrainn. Bhíodh an dreoilín marbh i gcónaí nach mór. Chítear dreamanna an dreoilín ag dul timpeall i láthair an lae inniu agus is fíorannamh a bhíonn dreoilín sa chrann acu. Gheibhtí an dreoilín an lá roimhe ré, nó b'fhéidir an oíche roimhe ré. Dheintí an dreoilín do mharú le buille bata agus b'fhuirist é do chur dá chois san oíche nuair a bheadh sé caoch ag neart solais. Bhí seanchas ag na daoine gurbh é an dreoilín a sceith ar an Slánaitheoir nuair a bhí sé ar theitheadh ós na Giúdaigh. Ag deireadh an lae chaithí an crann cuilinn agus an dreoilín isteach sa díog. Dá mbeadh rince an dreoilín ann chuirfí an crann ina sheasamh ag barr an tseomra mar chomhartha gur rince an dreoilín a bhíodh ann. Bhailíodh buachaillí an dreoilín ag crosaire éigin i lár an pharóiste, áit a bheadh oiriúnach do bhaill an dreoilín. Ní bhíodh aon tithe fé leith acu i dtosach báire ach thugaidís a n-aghaidh ar mhuintir tí a rug bua na féile leo ó dhúchas. Sheachnaídís tithe a mbíodh daoine dúra ina gcónaí iontu. De ghnáth, ní théidís ag triall ar thithe grabairí talún ná ar shíol na ndaoine sin mar bhíodh an sean-fhalla istigh don a leithéid. Is de shiúil a gcos a théidís, agus a théann, timpeall na dúiche i gcónaí. Sheinneadh na buachaillí gléasanna ceoil, leis. Ar na gléasanna sin áirítear veidhlín, orgán béil, feadóg agus fife. San tseanaimsir is gnáthach go mbíodh druma agus bodhrán ar iomchar acu, leis. Is port singil nó rince le céimeanna den tsaghas sin a dheintí. Gheibhtí agus geibhtear 2/ nó 2/6 ó na daoine ba fhlaithiúla ach réal nó scilling an gnáthairgead do na daoine aosta. Cúpla pingin a gheibheadh an dream óg ag gach tigh. Ní bhíodh aon fhear fé leith a bhíodh ina spáránaí ach thoghadh an lucht buín aon duine muiníneach a bheadh ina measc. Ag deireadh an lae roinntí an t-airgead go cothrom ar lucht an bhuín nó choimeádtaí an t-airgead do rince an Dreoilín. Is minic dá mbuailfeadh dhá bhuíon iasachta lena chéile, go mbuailfidís a chéile agus thabharfaidís drochíde ar a chéile, agus bheadh sé ina raic eatarthu nó go dteithfeadh dream amháin díobh.

[St Stephen's Day was, and is, a great day of sport and hunting. People like to get moving after overindulging on Christmas Day. The fowler goes fowling as St Stephen's Day falls during the season for it. People used to, and still do, go fox hunting. The hunt meets at the same place each year for drinks before taking off. It's said there used to be horse racing at Kiely's cross in the old days but now the followers of the sport go to the official race meetings in Limerick and in other places.

The 'Wren' goes from place to place on this day. Often, there are girls amongst the lads. Long ago they collected food and drink and maybe small sums of money from the big houses, and everything was divided among the poor. Money is what they gather nowadays and it's usually divided amongst the members of the 'Wren'. They used to wear whatever old clothes they'd get around the house, like old trousers, old dresses, old hats, or some outfit made from multi-coloured cotton. They'd often spend a week preparing for the occasion. Usually everyone wore a mask; often it was a bought mask, but sometimes it was made from a piece of cloth, rabbit skin or some other type of animal skin. The hats were decorated with ribbons and various ornaments. The decorated hats were a sight to behold. Each group of Wren Boys usually took a holly bush around with them; these were decorated with ribbons and coloured paper. The wren was placed on top of the bush, right in the middle. In most cases the wren was dead. Nowadays, the Wren Boys rarely have a wren in the bush. The wren was usually caught the day or night before. He was usually killed with a stick, and it was usually easy to knock him over at night when blinded with a strong light. It was believed that the wren betrayed our Saviour when he was fleeing the Jews.[2] At the end of the

day, the holly tree and the wren used to be thrown into the ditch. If there was a dance the tree would be put standing at the top of the room to show that it was the dance of the wren. The Wren Boys usually gathered at a crossroads in the middle of the parish, somewhere convenient for the participants. There were no particular houses they'd visit to start out with but they'd be sure to go to houses known for their generosity and they used to avoid houses known to be mean, and usually never go near the houses of land grabbers, nor their descendants, as the old boycott remained in place for their kind. They usually played musical instruments such as the violin, the mouthorgan, and the whistle and fife. Long ago, they usually had a drum or bodhrán with them. The Wren Boys often used to dance on the kitchen floor. They used to get, and still get, 2 shillings or 2 shillings 6 pence from the most generous people and a shilling was the amount normally given to the older members, with youngsters getting a couple of pence at each house. No man in particular used to act as purse-keeper but the group used to elect someone known to be honest from amongst the group. Often, if two groups from different places met up they would give each other a hiding, and there would be a right commotion until one of the groups fled.] (NFC 1088: 382-6; written by Tomás Ó Faoláin, Ring, County Waterford, 1947.)

Agnes Moran speaks of St Stephen's Day and the Wren Boys in Kilrush:

Very few, if any, ate meat on Stephen's day, and they used to say if you fasted from it on this day, you'd never die a lingering death. The one great sport that used to be was the Wren Boys, dressed up in all sorts of clothes, sacks and things, and they going around singing, dancing and doing tricks. Of course there used always be the young lads in the Wren, but fifty years ago in Kilrush there used to be the three or four big Wrens, with maybe as many as forty men in each. They had songs like these ones:

'The wren, the wren the king of all birds,
On Stephen's day was caught in the furze.
Up with the kettle, and down with the pan.
Give us a penny to bury the wren.'

Another wren song was:

'I killed the wren instead of a hen.
This time next year I'll kill it again.
Give us a copper to drink a toast.
Then we'll see who'll drink the most.'

They used to visit every house in the town and country, and come back to the town in the heel of the evening. They would collect and play at all the pubs, and very often 'twas a fight would happen if two bands of Wren Boys met. They used to have lively music – fiddles, mouthorgans, melodeons, and other instruments. They used to have their faces blackened with soot and paint, and a lot of

them used to have women's clothes on. They used to often carry a goat on a long lead with them or else one of them would dress up as a bear or wild beast, and he would be chasing all the youngsters all over the place. Of course the big thing here in the town was for the parade of the Temperance Hall Brass Band on Stephen's Day, and when they would be finishing up their parade, all the different Wrens they had met with used to fall in behind the band and sing, dance and shout, as they went their way. The man or men who kept the 'tokens' (money collected) were known as 'Bankers' and they divided it in shares in some pub, after the sport was all over. Very often members of Wren groups got invitations to go as *bacács*[3] to weddings coming off[4] in the area. (NFC 1391: 136-8; Agnes Moran (78), Kilrush, County Clare. Collector: Seán McGrath, January 1955.)

Interestingly, the collector, Seán McGrath, noted that the custom, as described by Agnes, had all but died out at the time of recording in 1955: 'This custom has practically faded away altogether now, except for a few youngsters, who wander around to collect a few shillings, but the days of the large "Wrens" are as dead in Kilrush as the custom of bull-baiting on St Stephen's day'.

Maura Scanlon provided this account from County Leitrim:

As regards St. Stephen's Day in the district, meat was abstained from on that day as a preventive against cattle

diseases. Even to this day some families never eat meat on this day, including my own. Wren Boys still go around the district but in smaller numbers than years ago. At present, five or six small boys dress in old clothes, nothing in particular except a straw hat, a bunch of feathers and a false face, sometimes made of cloth or paper. Their ages would range from ten to sixteen years. Years ago, as many as twenty used go together and the oldest member used generally be the *cisteoir*.[5] Sometimes they might have a shilling each to get. Six pence was the usual amount of money they got from each house. An old hat or bag was always carried by the *cisteoir* for the money. When the Wren Boys arrived at a house they always stated: 'Are the Wren Boys welcome?' and they then waited for 'Yes' or 'No.' I have never known an instance that they were refused admittance, they are generally always welcome. The first thing on arriving to a house was a recitation about the wren:

The wren, the wren, the king of all birds
And on St. Stephen's Day she is caught in the fir,
Although she's small and her family is great
Rise up, landlady and give us a treat.[6]
So up with the kettle and down with the pan
Give us our answer and let us be gone.

The answer was generally a few pence. A dance known as a half set always followed this and if any members could

sing in a changed voice, so their identity would not be known. Music was always a melodeon or a French fiddle.

This day was a great day for hunting in this district, not in large parties, but individuals used go to mountains after foxes with a gun and dog. This custom has also died out here. (NFC 1089: 182-3; Miss A.M. McGoldrick (50), Carrickmurray, County Leitrim. Collector: Maura Scanlon, June 1947.)

Kevin Danaher mentions bull-baiting amongst the pastimes associated with St Stephen's Day, and says it was a particular favourite in Leinster and Ulster.[7] In the material I have consulted it goes largely unmentioned, apart from the accounts collected by Seán McGrath in Kilrush, County Clare. At the time of collecting, bull-baiting wasn't known within living memory, with the custom said to have ended some 200 years previous. McGrath wrote the following note: 'Tadhg Kelly, Michael Carmody and Pat McMahon all told me about the following (bull-baiting), but none of them remember the custom itself. All their parents however, and Kelly's paternal grandfather, used to talk about such an occurrence. It stopped about the year 1780'. (NFC 1391: 139.)

Firstly, is the account of this custom from Tadhg Kelly:

You know Corney's Lane, below, well in there, they used to have a milk market about 200 years ago, and every St. Stephen's Day, they used have bull sports there. 'Twas how they used to bait a dead goose, and have it dipped in its own blood, and it tied onto an ash stick. Then two or four men would stand in the centre of the ring and pass the baited stick from one to the other, while the bull chased them. I did hear one time that the bull, one year, killed a fellow named Scannel or Scanian, by tossing him against the ground. But there's few who could tell you about it now.

Michael Carmody adds the following:

The bull-baiting was done away with about 200 years ago, as 'twas pagan-like, and then the local people were up against it. They used to have a square below at the back of Corney's Lane, where the old milk and butter market used to be, just at the back of Rush's bakery place now. 'Twas how they used a sort of pitch-fork, with a bit of red cloth dipped in blood tied to it, and the bull used to go chasing it and be stabbed by one of the fighters or 'Knoppers' as the challenge men used be called. They used to have money prizes for the bravest men, and a few were killed there. I don't think it was the Catholic clergy that stopped it, but no, I would be inclined to think it was the Protestant ministers as they owned that plot of ground, and the Protestants in those days were high and mighty. (NFC 1391: 139; Tadhg Kelly and Michael Carmody, Kilrush, County Clare. Collector: Seán McGrath, January 1955.)

the sun is finally gaining strength, with a noticeable stretch in the daylight. The poet Raifteirí famously sang of this moment: '*Anois teacht an Earraigh, beidh an lá ag dul chun síneadh, is tar éis na Féile Bríde, ardóidh mé mo sheol*' [Now the coming of spring, the days will lengthen, and after the festival of Bridget, I'll raise my sail].[1] In Scotland, as Kevin Danaher describes, 1 January had long been an important day of celebration: 'In Scotland, however, where Roman custom had long prevailed 1 January traditionally began the year and thus was of much importance in popular celebration; a Scottish origin for some of the custom associated with the day in Ireland might thus be sought.'[2]

With the arrival of a new year a sense of fear for the future pervades people's consciousness, with attempts at divination being at the core of many rituals. This rural society lived on the land, at the mercy of nature's whims, and many aspects of their lives, such as health and material security, were very much outside of their control. As Danaher puts it: 'Indeed, almost anything which happened on New Year's Eve and Day might be ominous of the future, and the nearer to the midnight hour when the year actually began, the more significant.'[3]

Among the fears deeply embedded in their psyche was the fear of hunger, with the spectre of the Great Famine of the 1840s ever-present. New Year's Eve was widely known as *Oíche na Coda Móire* (the Night of the Big Portion), and people often ate a very large meal in the belief that it would prevent any future scarcity of food. Also, a ritual was practiced whereby a cake of bread was banged against the door to banish hunger. As we have seen, the belief that water turned to wine at midnight was associated with Christmas Eve in some areas. This belief was also common in some areas on New Year's Eve, when it was believed Jesus turned water into wine at the wedding feast of Cana. It was believed that water in the well would also turn to wine on this night, with observance of the act being taboo. As we'll see, this belief was also widely associated with the night of the 5 January, the day before the feast of the Epiphany. The following account from west Kerry contains many of the traditional beliefs regarding New Year's Eve:

Oíche Choille nó 'Oíche na Coda Móire' a thugtar ar an oíche roimh Lá Caille. Bhíodh na coinnle ar lasadh an oíche sin, leis, is bhíodh cístí milse agus cístí rísíní déanta i gcomhair na hoíche mar a bhí i gcomhair Oíche Nollag. Bhíodh béile mór i gcomhair suipéir acu an oíche sin – iasc nó feoil agus práta a bhíodh de réir mar a d'fhéadfadh sé bheith acu. Deiridís leis na páistí óga a ndóthain a ithe mar ná gheobhaidís aon ghreim bídh ar feadh na bliana arís. Ní chuimhneodh na páistí gurb é an lá déanach den bhliain é, is dheinidís breoite iad féin ag ithe le heagla ná gheobhaidís aon rud le n-ithe ar feadh bliana. Sin í an chúis gur tugadh 'Oíche na Coda Móire' air.

Deirtí go ndeintí fíon den uisce ar a dó dhéag a chlog an oíche sin agus deirtear go raibh bean ann a chuaigh go tobar an oíche sin ag faire ar an bhfíon agus ní fheaca éinne as san amach í. An lá ina dhiaidh sin bhí gallán in aice an tobair in áit ná raibh aon chloch ná gallán riamh roimhe sin. Bhíodh mná an bhaile ag ní a gcuid éadaigh ar an gcloch san ina dhiaidh san, agus deirtear go raibh bean ann ina haonar lá is í ag bogadh na n-éadach le báisín ar an ngallán nuair a chuala sí an guth á rá: 'Ná buail mé, ná buail mé'. D'imigh sí as agus scanradh ina croí, is níor nigh éinne aon éadach ar an ngallán as san amach.

Oíche Choille bhíodh sé de nós acu is atá fós bollóg rísíní ná bíodh aon smut bainte as a thabhairt don té ab óige a bheadh sa tigh dá mbeadh aon chaint in aon chor aige, is dheineadh sé an bhollóg a bhualadh ar an ndoras thoir agus a rá: 'Fógraím gaoth aniar ar na Sasanaigh ó anocht go dtí bliain ó anocht.' É sin a rá trí huaire is é ag bualadh na bollóige ar an ndoras i gcónaí, is nuair a bheadh an méid sin ráite aige mant a bhaint as an mbollóg lena bhéal. Bhíodh na héinne ag faire ar an ngaoth an mhaidin ina dhiaidh san, is dá mbeadh sí anoir bheadh an bhliain sin leis na Sasanaigh, is dá mbeadh sí aniar bheadh sí leis na hÉireannaigh. Tar éis an rósairí a rá an oíche sin deireadh ceann an tí an phaidir seo: 'Beirimid buíochas do Dhia i dtaobh na bliana seo atá caite againn. Go leanfaidh Dia is leis an Maighdean Mhuire gura fearra a thosnóimid is a chríochnóimid an bhliain atá chugainn i gcaidreamh, i ngrásta, i saol is i sláinte, i gcabhair is i gcúnamh ar an Maighdean Mhuire is a haon Mhac trócaireach anocht.'

Chaitheadh na héinne an phaidir seo a rá chomh maith le fear an tí, is dá mbé an leanbh sa chliabhán féin é, chuiridís a lámha le chéile an fhaid is a bheadh na daoine eile á rá.

[New Year's Eve, or 'The Night of the Big Portion,' was the night before New Year's Day. The candles were lit on this night, and sweet cakes and raisin cakes were made just like on Christmas Eve. They used to have a large supper, with fish or meat and potato, depending on what was feasible. They would tell the children to eat their fill as they wouldn't get another bite for a year. The children wouldn't remember it was the last day of the year and they'd make themselves sick for fear they wouldn't get another morsel for a year. That's why it was called 'The Night of the Big Portion.'

The water apparently turned to wine on this night at 12.00. It is said that a woman went to the well to observe the wine on this night and was never seen again. The next day there was a pillar next to the well where there had

never been a pillar or stone before. Women used to wash their clothes on this stone after that, and it's said that a woman was there on her own one day when she heard a voice saying: 'Don't hit me, don't hit me.' It frightened the heart out of her and she took off, and nobody ever washed clothes on that stone again.

On New Year's Eve night it was, and still is, the custom to give a loaf of raisin bread, with no bite taken out of it, to the youngest in the house if he had any speech at all. He would then beat the loaf against the front door, saying: 'I summon the west wind on the English from tonight until a year from tonight.' This was said three times, all the while beating the loaf against the door, and once he had that much said he would take a scelp of the bread in his mouth. Everybody used to observe the wind the next day. If the wind was blowing from the east it would be the year of the English, but if it was from the west it would be on the side of the Irish.

After saying the rosary that night the head of the house would say the following prayer: 'We give thanks to God for the year just passed. May it be God's and the Virgin Mary's will that we shall better begin and end the next year in our relations with one another, in grace, in life and health, in help and assistance to the Virgin Mary and her merciful Son tonight.' Everybody had to say this prayer as well as the man of the house and if there was an infant in the cradle, they would join his hands together while

everybody else was praying.] (NFC 217: 141-4; Máire
Bean Uí Ghrifín (74), Kinard, County Kerry, Collector:
Seosamh Ó Grifín, July 1928.)

The following account is also from west Kerry:

*Bíonn suipéar mór ins gach tigh agus itheann gach éinne a
dhóthain, mar ná beidh faic le n-ithe aige i mbliana arís.
Cuireann gach líon tí trí bhuicéad mhóra d'fhíoruisce ar
bhord sa chistin in onóir na hoíche a deineadh fíon den uisce
fadó. Coimeádann siad braon as gach buicéad le haghaidh na
bliana chun trí deora a thabhairt d'éinne den líon tí a bheidh
breoite. Téann an duine is óige den líon tí go dtí an doras agus
císte aráin (gan aon ghreim a bheith as). Buaileann sé an císte
i gcoinnibh an dorais trí n-uaire agus deireann: 'Fógraím an
gorta go Tír na dTurcach, anocht agus bliain ó anocht agus
anocht féin go fírinneach.'*

[Each household gathers for a big supper with
everybody eating their fill, as they will not get any more
for the remainder of the year. Each house puts three large
buckets of spring water on the kitchen table in honour
of the night when water was turned into wine long ago.
A drop is kept from each bucket for the coming year and
3 drops given to anybody who'll get sick. The youngest
member of the household goes to the door with a cake of
bread (with no bite taken from it), and he beats it against
the door three times, and says: 'I summon the hunger to
the Land of the Turks, tonight and a year from tonight,

and tonight itself truthfully.'] (NFC 22, 449-50; written by
Eibhlín Ní Mhurchadha (16), Ballydavid, County Kerry,
August 1932.)

In Donegal, Niall Ó Dubhthaigh has a tale regarding the
water turning to wine on New Years' Eve, which he claims
to have heard from a witness to the event:

*Níor chuala mé trácht ariamh ar uisce a thabhairt isteach
Oíche Nollag Mór nó a dhath mar sin, ach tá sé 'na ghnás
anseo an t-uisce a thabhairt isteach roimh luí gréine Oíche
Nollag Beag (Oíche Choille). Bhí mé ag caint le fear a fuair
taispeánadh maith mór fá seo i Leitir Ceanainn in am. Bhí sé
maslaithe as miosúr ag obair agus nuair a tháinig sé ina bhaile
ba mhaith leis a chosa a ní. Bhí sé féin agus a mháthair ag
stopadh in aon teach amháin. Bhí sise aosta go measartha agus
bhí tobar beag acu thíos i gcúl an tí. D'iarr seisean braon uisce
te go nífeadh sé a chosa. Dúirt sí go raibh sí buartha nach raibh
aon ndeor uisce istigh, go dearna sí neamart agus faillí, agus
gur seo Oíche Nollag Beag agus nár mhaith léi a dhul amach fá
choinne uisce. D'aithin sí go maith go raibh sórt feirge air agus
dar léi féin, nuair a chonaic sí goidé mar a bhí sé á ghlacadh, go
dtabharfadh sí isteach an t-uisce cá bith. Chuaigh sí amach fán
a choinne agus nuair a tháinig sí isteach chuaigh sí á dhortadh
amach ar an scála, agus ansin chonaic an bheirt acu goidé a
bhí ann. Bhí sé díreach cosúil leis an fhíon a ba dheise a chonaic
siad ariamh, agus cha ndearna sí ach a chur isteach ins an
stópa ar ais agus a fhágáil amuigh ins an áit a bhfuair sí é.*

THE NEW YEAR AND EPIPHANY

*Chreid seisean ón oíche sin go dtí lá a bháis go n-athraíonn an
t-uisce Oíche Nollag Beag. Tá cuntas cinnte gur Oíche Nollag
Beag a rinneadh an chéad mhíorúilt agus deirtear gur sin an
fáth a n-athraíonn an t-uisce ins na toibreacha an oíche sin.*

[I never heard mention of water being taken in on
Christmas Eve or anything like that, but it is the custom
here to bring in the water before sunset on New Year's Eve.
I was talking to a man who saw this happen in Letterkenny
one time. He was worn out from work and when he came
home he wanted to wash his feet. He and his mother lived
in the same house. She was quite old and they had a small
well at the back of the house. He asked for a drop of hot
water so he could wash his feet. She apologised for not
having any water inside, she had been remiss, but seeing
as it was New Year's Eve she didn't want to go outside for
water. She noticed he was a bit angry about this, and given
the way he felt, she brought in the water. She went out to
collect it and when she poured it into a bowl they saw what
was there. It was just like the nicest wine they had ever
seen, and all she did was put it back into the flagon and
left it out in the place where she got it. From that moment
until the day he died, he believed that the water changed
on New Year's Eve. There is a definite account that the first
miracle took place on New Year's Eve, and this is why they
say the water in the wells changes on this night.] (NFC
932: 415-6; Niall Ó Dubhthaigh (69) with help from his
sister, Eibhlín, Cloghaneely, County Donegal. Collector:
Seán Ó hEochaidh, 1943.)

The following is another cautionary tale, from Donegal,
regarding the water turning to wine on New Year's Eve:

Bhí Oíche Nollag Beag ina saoire fosta ó dhul ó sholas go ham
codlata. Ba seo an oíche dheireanach sa bhliain. Ar an oíche seo

ní thógfaí braon uisce as an tobar tar éis luí gréine. An méid uisce a bheadh a dhíth fá choinne na hoíche agus na maidine, bheirfí isteach roimh luí na gréine é. Ní hamháin go dtabharfaí isteach an t-uisce ach ní chaithfí uisce ar bith amach ach oiread, salach nó glan; d'fhágfaí istigh go maidin é. Ba é cothrom an oíche seo a thiontaigh ár Slánaitheoir an t-uisce ina fhíon ag an mbainis i gCana nuair a reath an fhíon gann. Is le móronóir a thabhairt do Mhac Dé ar son na míorúiltí a rinne sé ba chúis leis an ghnás seo. Chreid an uile dhuine dá ndéanfadh siad athrú go dtiocfadh scrios ó lámh Dé orthu. Bhí fear ann nár ghéill don ghnás seo agus chuaigh sé chun tobair ach níor phill sé; ar maidin fuarthas marbh é le taobh an bhuicéid uisce ar bhruach an tobair. Bean eile nár ghéill don ghnás ach oiread, agus thug sí isteach uisce i ndiaidh luí na gréine. Chuaigh sí ar ais ionsar an tobar fá choinne buicéid eile ag uair an mheán oíche ach an iarraidh seo ní raibh a dhath uisce le fáil aici nó bhí an tobar ina fhuil. Bhuail eagla í, ach ní raibh sí ábalta corraí as áit na mbonn. D'amharc sí suas agus chonaic sí spiorad os cionn an tobair a dúirt léi: 'nach bhfuil a fhios agat gurb é cothrom an oíche seo a d'athraigh ár Slánaitheoir an t-uisce go fíon.' Chuir an bhean ceist: 'cad chuige a raibh an tobar ina fhuil?' Freagraíodh í go mbíonn sin amhlaidh i dtólamh ag uair an mheán oíche má thógtar uisce i ndiaidh gabháil faoi den ghrian; an teaghlach a thógfas an t-uisce go dtarraingíonn siad fuil Íosa Críost. Ó seo anuas, coinníodh an gnás go dúthrachtach ach mar an uile shórt, rinneadh dearmad de le linn ama.

[New Year's Eve was also a holiday from sunset until bedtime. This was the last night of the year. On this night not a drop of water would be taken from the well after sunset. Any water needed from night until morning would be brought in before the sun went down. Not only would the water not be brought in, but no water would be thrown out either, dirty or clean; it would stay inside until morning. It was on this night that our Saviour turned water into wine at the wedding feast of Cana when the wine became scarce. This custom was observed to honour the miracle of the Son of God. Everybody believed that if they changed this practice they would be destroyed by the hand of God. There was a man who didn't adhere to this custom and he went to the well but he didn't return, and he was found dead the following morning next to the bucket at the side of the well. There was also a woman who didn't follow this custom and she brought in the water after sunset. She went back to the well for another bucket at midnight but this time there was no water, just a blood-filled well. Fear came over her and she remained rooted to the spot. She looked up and saw a spirit above the well who said to her: 'do you not know that it was on this night that our Saviour changed the water into wine.' The woman asked why the well was now turned to blood? She was answered and told this always happened if water was taken from the well after sunset. The household who takes water draws the blood of Christ. From then on the custom was steadfastly adhered to, but like everything it was forgotten with the passage of time.] (NFC 335: 138-40; Bríghid Ní Aghartaigh (30), Kilcar, County Donegal. Collector: Anna Ní Éigheartaigh, March 1936.)

THE NEW YEAR AND EPIPHANY

The following account from Kilrush, County Clare provides us with a variety of beliefs associated with New Year's Eve:

> My mother used to tell us that in her young days the people who lived all around them, used to leave a fresh jug of well water on the table, in the hope that it would be either blessed or turned into wine during the night. This was done mainly by women who had sons who they wanted to make priests of. The curtains or shades in some houses used to be thrown back [closed] for five minutes before the new year came in always, as 'twas thought that the bad spirits of the old year, that may have been within a house, especially in a house where death or misfortune had been during the past year. The shades or blinds were drawn so as to let such evil out, as spirits would not leave if a window was bare. Of course 'twas on New Year's Eve that the women used to be watching the candles in case they would spill or burn crooked. If this happened it meant a death would occur in the house during the coming year. If men were in any house and twelve midnight struck on the clock, they were always supposed to stand up and take off their hats or caps, and say: 'God speed it now, and God bless the new one'. (NFC 1391: 143; Tone O'Dea, Kilrush, County Clare. Collector: Seán McGrath, January 1955.)

New Year's Day

As a new year dawned, the future was approached with
some trepidation. The observance of signs or omens was
the order of the day; and the weather was one way of
seeing into the coming year:

> *Agus bhí piseoga an domhain ag na glúinte a bhí anseo
> romhainn i dtaobh an lá seo, ceann nó dhó ná 'fuil imithe ar
> fad fós. Seo ceann acu: Dá n-éiríodh na tuillte le báisteach ag
> teacht isteach don bhliain nua, d'éiríodh aontaí agus margaí
> na bliana sin agus bheadh an saol fé shonas, ach dá gurbh
> amhlaidh bheadh na huiscí ag titim, nó na habhainnte tirim
> níor chomhartha maith ar bith é sin ar an sonas a bheadh ar
> aontaí ná margaí an bhliain sin.*

[The older generations had so many superstitions
regarding this day, one or two of them are still with us. The
following is one: If the rivers were flooded at the beginning
of the new year it meant the prices at fairs and markets
would rise, and life would bring good fortune, but if the
waters were falling, or the rivers dry, this wasn't a good
sign that the fairs and markets would bring prosperity.]
(NFC 40: 206; written by Seán Mac Mathghamhna (57),
Doolin, County Clare, 1934.)

Amhlaoibh Ó Loingsigh also mentions the floods, along
with wind direction:

Lá Caille, an chéad lá d'Eanáir, chuireadh seandaoine suim sa mhaidin seo. Dá mbeadh uisce mór san abhainn níos airde ná mar ba ghnáth, b'sheo comhartha a bhíodh acu go mbeadh nithe an-dhaor an bhliain sin, nó dá mbeadh an ghaoth anoir deiridís go mbeadh an bhliain i bhfabhar an tSasanaigh. Agus ba chuma cad é an áit eile 'na mbeadh sí, chreididís go mbeadh sí fábhrúil leo féin.

[The old people were interested in New Year's Day. If the water in the river was higher than usual, this was a sign that things would be very dear that year, or if there was an east wind that the year would be with the English; and it didn't matter from whatever other direction it blew, it would favour themselves.] (NFC 1084: 219; Amhlaoibh Ó Loingsigh (72), Coolea, County Cork. Collector: Cáit Uí Liatháin, December 1944.)

The morning of New Year's Day was a time of superstitious rituals, such as the following from Tone O'Dea, in Kilrush: 'The ashes were not removed at all on New Year's Day, and as long as there was a boy or man in the house, 'twas always a man set, and lit the fire on New Year's morning.' (NFC 1391: 143; Tone O'Dea, Kilrush, County Clare. Collector: Seán McGrath, January 1955.)

Niall Ó Dubhthaigh remembers a ritual from County Donegal:

Ag éirí don teaghlach ar maidin Lá Nollag Beag, agus iad ag teacht aníos agus ag teacht anuas as na seomraí, bheadh an mháthair ansin agus soitheach uisce coisricthe ar an tábla aici agus d'ólfadh achan nduine den teaghlach é. Ba é an chiall a bhí acu le seo a dhéanamh le tús maith a chur ar an mbliain úr, agus le Dia achan rath a chur orthu ar feadh na bliana úire. Nuair a thiocfadh duine ar bith isteach Lá na Bliana Úire, comharsa nó stráinséir, déarfadh achan nduine: 'Go mbeannaí Dia sa teach, go gcuire Dia bliain úr shona rathúil chugaibh agus go dtuga Dia bliain úr rathúil díbh uilig agus go sábhála sé sibh féin agus bhur dteaghlach ar achan chaill agus urchóid, agus go raibh sibh uilig beo ins na grása is mó.'

[When the family rose on New Year's Day morning, the mother of the house would have a container of holy water on the table and each person would drink from it. This was done to ensure a good start to the year and that God would let them prosper throughout the new year. When anybody came in on New Year's Day, whether a neighbour or a stranger, everybody would say: 'May God bless the house and may God send a happy and prosperous year to you, and may God give you a successful New Year and may he save you and all your household from every loss and harm, and may you all live in the graces.'] (NFC 932: 486; Niall Ó Dubhthaigh, Cloghaneely, County Donegal. Collector: Seán Ó hEochaidh, 1943.)

Mrs Wilson, from Drumderg, County Longford spoke of the following: 'On New Year's Day, get up early, dig three sods in the name of the Trinity and you'll have a profitable season and be first in with your crops.' (NFC 80: 19; Mrs

Wilson, Drumderg, County Longford. Collector: Máire
Ní Chárthaigh, 1929/30.)

On the morning of New Year's Day great emphasis
was placed on who the first to enter the house was. This,
again, would reveal whether good luck or bad would rule
the coming year. Women were particularly ostracised on
the morning of New Year's Day: 'No woman was supposed
to be the first to wish one a Happy New Year, whether
she had red, black or white hair.' (NFC 1391: 144; Tone
O'Dea, Kilrush, County Clare. Collector Seán McGrath,
January 1955.)

Niall Ó Dubhthaigh gives a strongly worded account of
this belief:

*Deir siad i dtólamh go bhfuil sé go mór níos ádhúla fear a
theacht isteach maidin Lá Nollag Beag nó bean. Is cuma á
dheiseacht nó á chaoithiúlacht an bhean, nó is cuma leobhtha
á fheabhas í; déarfaidh siad i gcónaí gur fearr leo an fear a
fheiceáil ag teacht isteach, agus go háirid dá dtigfeadh bean rua
chostarnocht isteach ar an chéad dhuine chun tí, bheadh sé go
díreach chomh maith leo, go sábhála Dia muid, diabhal Ifrinn a
fheiceáil a' tarraingt orthu. Bheadh intinn acu gur tús mí-áidh
agus achan rud a ba mheasa nó a chéile a bheadh ann dá
bhfeicfeadh siad an bhean rua a' tarraingt ar an teach acu Lá
Nollag Beag. Agus leoga, coinnigh cuimhne air nach raibh bróga
ar mhórán cailíní ins na laethaibh a bhfuil mé ag trácht orthu.*

[They always say that it is far luckier to have a man
come in on New Year's Day morning than a woman. It
doesn't matter how attractive or pleasant she is, it matters

little how great she is; they will always say they prefer to see a man coming in. If a barefoot, red-haired woman was the first to the house, it was the same to them as seeing the devil from hell heading their way. God save us; it would be an unlucky start to the year, with everything worse than the next in store, if they saw a red-haired woman approach. And remember, that there weren't many girls with shoes in the days I'm speaking of.] (NFC 932: 497-8; Niall Ó Dubhthaigh, Cloghaneely, County Donegal. Collector: Seán Ó hEochaidh, 1943.)

The following account is from Doolin, County Clare:

Agus bhí piseoga an domhain ag na seandaoine bhí anseo i dtaobh an chéad duine thiocfadh isteach chucu an chéad lá do bhliain. Bhí daoine ann agus bhíodh sé mar ainm orthu go leanfadh ádh agus sonas aon té a raghaidís isteach ann roimh éinne eile an chéad lá do bhliain. Agus bhí daoine eile a raibh sé mar ainm orthu mar nárbh fhearrde muintir an tí sin an bhliain dá mbeidís ar an gcéad dhuine a chuirfeadh cois thar an dtairseach an chéad lá do bhliain. Is amhlaidh do chuirtí cuireadh don té a raibh ainm an rathúnais air teacht ar an gcéad dhuine ar an gcéad lá, agus nuair a thiocfadh ní miste a rá go mbeadh fáilte gheal roimh an nduine sin agus gloine mhaith biotáille, nó b'fhéidir péire acu sin. Ach 'sé an doras dúnta bhí le fáil ag an nduine mírathúil a raibh an drochainm air dá dtagadh sé. Agus maidir le mná, ní raibh glaoch ar bith orthu a theacht isteach in aon teach cónaithe lasmuigh dá dteach féin an lá sin.

THE NEW YEAR AND EPIPHANY

[The old people had a lot of superstitions as regards the first person calling in on the first day of the year. There were some people who had the reputation of bringing luck to whoever they'd call into before anybody else on the first day. Others could expect a bad year if certain people crossed the threshold on New Year's Day. It seems people known to bring prosperity would receive an invitation to be the first person in the door, and, needless to say, they got a fine welcome, as well as one, or maybe two drops of strong drink. The door would be closed on anybody with a name for misfortune should they arrive.] (NFC 40: 207; written by Seán Mac Mathghamhna (57), Doolin, County Clare, 1934.)

We've seen the tradition of not beginning any work and its association with 28 December. In the following from Seán Mac Mathghamhna he recalls a manifestation of this tradition on New Year's Day:

Bhí a lán pisreoga againn i dtaobh chorraí na cré an Chéad Lá do Bhliain ná an chéad Luan don bhliain. Dá mbeadh corp le cur i dtalamh an Chéad Lá do Bhliain is amhlaidh a chaithfí an uaigh a dhéanamh an lá roimhe sin le heagla lomadh na bliana a tharraingt ar mhuintir an tí sin, ach níor dhíobháil an chré a chur ar an gcorp ó bhí sé caite aníos an lá roimhe sin. Agus ar an nós céanna bhí tóir mhór ag an seandream i suathadh na hithreach an chéad Luan do bhliain. Bhí beirt nó triúr againn ag obair i gcoill ar an lá sin i gcaitheamh do bhlianta ó shoin.

Níor dhream pisreogach sinn agus níor chuir sinn aon nath ins an lá a bhí ann thar aon lá eile. I gceann tamaill tháinig seanfhear chugainn agus ón nós ar labhair sé linn, nuair a chonaic sé sinn ag luascadh na cré, ba dhóigh leat go raibh sinn ciontach i gceann de na Deich n-Aitheanta. Ach bhí lá na linne sin agus an saol sin gairid a bheith imithe, agus is ró-ghearr ná beadh tuairisc orthu féin ná ar na pisreoga úd do ghéilleadar dóibh ina lá féin. D'imigh an lá sin agus tháinig an lá seo.

[We had a lot of superstitions regarding the turning of the sod, on the first day of the year or on the first Monday of the year. If a corpse had to be buried on the first, the grave would have to be dug the day before to avoid bringing a year of misfortune on the household, but it was fine to put the earth on the corpse once the grave had been dug the day before. Similarly, the old people kept a keen eye on any disturbance of the soil on the first Monday of the year. Some years ago, on a particular day, two or three of us were working in the wood. We weren't superstitious and we didn't give any thought to what day it was over any other. After a while an old man approached us and spoke to us when he saw us turning the soil; you'd swear we were guilty of breaking one of the Ten Commandments. But, the times were changing and that life was beginning to fade, and it wouldn't be long before there'd be no more mention of the superstitions that were abided by before. That day went and this day came.] (NFC 40: 208; written by Seán Mac Mathghamhna (57), Doolin, County Clare, 1934.)

The Epiphany

On 6 January, The Epiphany, to give its ecclesiastical title, is celebrated. In Ireland it is still known as 'Little Christmas' or 'Women's Christmas'. In Irish it was known as '*Lá Nollag Beag*', or '*Nollaig na mBan*'. In Donegal, as we've seen, '*Lá Nollag Beag*' referred to New Year's Day, with the 6th being called '*Achar an Dá Lá Dhéag*'. In traditional society the night of the fifth was an important night, known in some places as 'Little Christmas Night', and in Irish, *Oíche na dTrí Ríthe* ('The Night of Three Kings'). In Donegal it was called *Nollaig an Dá Choinneal Déag* ('Christmas of the Twelve Candles').

Máire Ní Fhearghaill explains the origins of the Women's Christmas as told to her:

> Little Christmas was called the Women's Christmas because it was believed that the women were in the majority at the Wedding Feast of Cana, and because it was a woman, our Blessed Lady, that caused the miracle to be worked, thereby prolonging the feast. It was believed that the women should have this time each year set aside for their special rejoicing. Of course it is a common belief that the water is still changed into wine on Little Christmas Night. That is why you should always have a bucket of clean water inside and the floor swept before going to bed that night. This water was never used though in the morning. (NFC 1084: 198; Máire Ní Fhearghaill (83), Drimoleague, County Cork. Collector: Éamon Mac Firbhisigh, December 1944.)

Máire Bean Uí Ghrifín speaks of the Women's Christmas: '*Thugaidís Nollaig na mBan air, leis, is deiridís ná bíodh aon mhaith sa Nollaig sin: "Nollaig na mban, Nollaig an mheath, Nollaig na bhFear, Nollaig mhór mhaith".*' [They used to call it the Women's Christmas as well, but they used to say that there wasn't much good in it: 'The Women's Christmas, the dregs of Christmas. The Men's Christmas, the big Christmas of plenty']. (NFC 217: 144; Máire Bean Uí Ghrifín (74), Kinard, County Kerry. Collector: Seán Ó Grifín, July 1938.)

Mary Walshe recounts the ritual of lighting the candles on the fifth and sixth:

> Then for '*Nollaig na mBan*' another set used be lit, and they used to be burned out early, as they used to light these on the eve of *Nollaig na mBan*, but on the day of *Nollaig na mBan* itself my father used to light the candles about 3 o'clock in the evening, so that they'd be burned out by the time he went to bed. He often stopped up until a way after midnight, waiting for them to burn out, as he was superstitious about they not being burned before the twelfth night. (NFC 1391: 129; Mary Walshe, Kilrush, County Clare. Collector: Seán McGrath, January 1955)

Bríghid Ní Aghartaigh from Donegal gives this account of the night of the fifth:

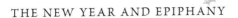

'Achar an Dá Lá Dhéag' mar bheir corr-dhuine air; 'sé seo an seisiú lá de mhí an Eanáir. Thugtaí Nollaig an Dá Choinneal Déag ar an lá roimhe seo. Is cosúil go raibh trí Nollaig acu sa tsean-am. I dtús ama bhí gach uile lá ó Lá Nollag Mór go dtí an seisiú lá den bhliain úr ina lá saoire na hEaglaise. Bhuel, ní raibh tuataí ábalta saoire a choinneáil ar an oiread seo laetha agus cuireadh deireadh leo ach gur fágadh an seisiú ina shaoire le cruthú go raibh dhá shaoire dhéag ann i dtús ama. Bhí sé de ghnás ag na Caitlicigh dhá choinneal déag a lasadh, agus a ndó i gcoinne na bhfuinneogaí, ar an seisiú oíche den bhliain úr. Ghníodh siad seo i gcuimhne ar an dá shaoire dhéag. Bhí cuid eile á rá gur le honóir do na hApstail a lasfaí na coinnle.

[The Epiphany as some people called it, this being the 6th of January. They used to call the day before the 'Christmas of the Twelve Candles'. It appears that in the old days there were three Christmases. In the beginning every day from Christmas Day until the sixth day of the new year was a Church holiday. Well, the country people weren't able to keep a holiday over that many days and they were all removed, apart from the sixth, which remained a holiday to show that there had been twelve days at the beginning. It was the custom for Catholics to light twelve candles and burn them in the window on the sixth night of the new year. They used to do this in memory of twelve holidays. Others said they were lit in honour of the twelve apostles.] (NFC 335: 141-2; Bríghid Ní Aghartaigh (30), Kilcar, County Donegal. Collector: Anna Ní Éigheartaigh, March 1936.)

Amhlaoibh Ó Loingsigh remembers the following superstition, and tale, associated with the night of the 5th:

Oíche Nollag Beag nó Oíche na dTrí Ríthe: creididís go mbíodh uair na hachainí tráth éigin den oíche sin, ach n'fheadar éinne cad é an t-am d'oíche. Bhíodh scéalta acu ar sheanmhnaoi; d'fhan sí suas in aice na teine agus an achainí aici á hiarraidh coitianta. B'é an rud a bhí aici á rá: 'A Thiarna, dein iarla dem mhac.' Do léim cat a bhí ann in airde ar an driosúr, do leag anuas báisín agus dhein smidiríní dhi ar an urlár. 'Go mbrise an diabhal do chosa mar chat,' ar sise. B'shid é díreach nuair a bhí uair na hachainí ann agus thit an cat lena cheithre cosa briste; 'sé seo bhí aici in ionad iarla bheith déanta den mhac.

[They used to believe that there was a wishing hour at some stage during the night, but nobody knows at exactly what time. They had stories about an old woman who waited up by the fire making a wish regularly. This is what she said: 'Oh Lord, make an earl of my son.' A cat jumped on the dresser, knocked over a basin, making smithereens of it. 'Cat, may the devil break your legs,' she said. That was just when the wishing hour struck and the cat fell to the floor with his four legs broken. That was what she received instead of her son being made into an earl.] (NFC 1084: 220; Amhlaoibh Ó Loingsigh (72), Coolea, County Cork. Collector: Cáit Uí Liatháin, March 1945.)

Henry Evanson from Schull in County Cork recounts a cautionary tale regarding the phenomenon of water turning to wine:

> On Little Christmas Night [the night of 5 January] all water, both indoors and outdoors, according to popular belief turned into wine about midnight. No one liked to remain up out of bed as long on that night as all the other nights of the Christmas season, for it was firmly believed that a young girl whose curiosity overcame her, stayed up all night, tasting the water from time to time to prove for herself the truth of the popular belief that the water turned into wine sometime during the night, but she was found dead next morning. (NFC 1084: 180; Denis Keohane (71), Mrs Maria O'Regan (65), Mrs Anglin (60), Schull, County Cork. Collector: Henry Evanson, March 1945.)

Sarah O'Hark, from Dromintee, County Armagh recalls a custom practised in her mother-in-law's house on the Twelfth Night:

> Well, I never did hear of Wee Christmas. Oh aye, I heard of the Twelve Days. All I mind about the Twelfth Day was what the oul'[4] woman that was here, Barney's mother, God be good to them all, would do. She was from Carrickasticken (Dromintee Parish). Maybe they do it out there still. Wee Barney Callan was here at the time, and she had him schooled. The Twelfth Night she made Barney go

out and take in a shovel of cow dung, and put it on the middle of the floor. And she had her twelve resin candles ready, and stuck them round in the dung. And then when they all gathered in (came in from foddering)[5] we all knelt down and said the rosary. (NFC 1087: 128; Sarah O'Hark (70), Dromintee, County Armagh. Collector: Michael J. Murphy, December 1944.)

Niall Ó Dubhthaigh remembers the traditional fair held on the sixth in Gortahork, County Donegal:

Achar an Dá Lá Dhéag an t-ainm a thugtar ariamh anall ar an lá saoire sin a bhíos ann ar an 6ú lá d'Eanáir. Tá baile beag ann a dtabharann siad Gort a'Choirce air, agus bíonn aonach ansin ar an seisú lá de gach mí sa bhliain, agus tarlaíonn sé go dtiteann Achar an Dá Lá Dhéag ar an seiseamh lá, agus fágann sin cruinniú mór daoine i dtólamh i nGort a' Choirce ar an lá sin. Bíonn an baile pacáilte le daoine as achan chearn, agus tá mé ag inse duit gur sin an lá a ghníos tithe Ghort a' Choirce a gcuid fómhair. Díolann na tithe óstaigh achan deor biotáilte nó pórtair le fáil iontu. Ins an am a chuaigh thart ba ghnáthach le cuid mhór lucht siúil a bheith ag dul thart a' díol neithe – bróga agus éadaigh agus achan sórt ar an tsaol dá dtiocfadh liom a ainmniú. Níl aon phéas ar an taobh seo den chontae nach gcaithfeadh a theacht ann sa tsean-am le smacht agus riail a choinneáil ar an scaifte iontach daoine a bhíodh ansin. D'óladh cuid den dream seo a thigeadh chun aonaigh an lá sin braon, barraíocht agus leoga cha raibh sé furast á gcoinneáil suaimhneach. Bhí sé ina ghnás anseo

*go dtí tá tuairim ar dheich mbliana fichead ó shoin: an cailín a
bheadh a' caint le buachaill, agus a mbeadh rún pósta acu, mar a
déarfá, bhí sé ina ghnás acu san am sin go gcasfaí an bheirt acu ar
a chéile ar an aonach tráthnóna Achar an Dá Lá Déag.*

[The 6th of January was always a festival day. There's
a small town called Gortahork and a fair is held there on
the 6th of every month during the year. As the Epiphany
falls on the 6th, it means a large crowd of people gather
here on this date. The town is packed with people from all
over, and I'm telling you, the houses of Gortahork make
their money. The pubs sell every drop of strong drink
and porter they have. In times past the travelling people
would go around selling stuff like shoes and clothes and
more besides, if I could name them. All the police officers
from this part of the county had to come in the old days to
keep order amongst the huge crowd assembled. A certain
amount of them would drink too much and it wasn't
easy keep them calm. It was a custom here up to 30 years
ago that a girl and boy, intending to marry, would meet
up at the fair on the afternoon of the Epiphany.] (NFC
932: 503-5; Niall Ó Dubhthaigh, Cloghaneely, County
Donegal. Collector: Seán Ó hEochaidh, 1943.)

The Festival Ends

In the modern Christmas, keeping decorations up until
6 January is still the custom, though not strictly observed.

In traditional society customs regarding the taking down of decorations were rigidly observed, though regional variation is evident:

Bhíodh an Nollaig caite nuair a bhíodh Lá Nollag Beag imithe ach ní thógaidís an cuileann ná an eidheann anuas go ceann naoi lá ina dhiaidh san. Deiridís nár cheart é a thógaint anuas roimhe sin, is ní thógfadh daoine eile anuas é go dtí Domhnach Cásca. Is cuma leo anois cathain a thógann siad anuas é is tógann cuid acu anuas é an lá i ndiaidh Lae Nollag Beag.

[Once the Little Christmas passed the festival of Christmas was over, though the holly and ivy wouldn't be taken down for another nine days. It was said that it should never be taken down before this. Some people wouldn't take them down until Easter Sunday. They don't care nowadays when they take them down, with some taking them down the day after the Little Christmas.] (NFC 217: 144; Máire Bean Uí Ghrifín (74), Kinard, County Kerry. Collector: Seosamh Ó Grifín, July 1928.)

Mrs Leonard from Delvin in County Westmeath speaks of taking down the decorations: 'In some houses, decorations were burned the day after the Twelfth Day. In others they were not removed 'till after Candlemas, and sometimes were kept until Shrove and burned under the pancakes.' (NFC 1085: 94; Mrs Leonard (93), Delvin, County Westmeath, 1945.)

Mrs McCarthy in County Cork describes the custom she followed:

> *Mhuise*, we keeps up the ould custom an' don't take down the holly an' ivy till Shrove Tuesday night an put it bakin' the pancakes. I don't know, alay, what's the manin[6] of it. I used to see the ould people doin' it an' we're keeping up the ould custom – that's the way with us. (NFC: 462; 228–9; Mrs McCarthy (62), Enniskean, County Cork. Collector: Diarmuid Ó Cruadhlaoich, January 1938.)

From Kilrush, County Clare comes the following:

> Holly was left up till the morning after Little Christmas, when it was taken down and burned immediately in the kitchen fire, by whoever was lighting the fire that morning. Lots of people used to keep the palm and a sprig of *seamróg*[7] and then on the day after the Little Christmas, they used to tie the three plants together, and burn them in the fire. This was done for the sake of preventing another famine in west Clare, and was supposed to have been started after the terrible famine of 1847.[8] (NFC 1391: 124–5; Mrs Mary Walshe /Batt Shea, Kilrush, County Clare. Collector: Seán McGrath, January 1955.)

Notes

Introduction

1 Ó Giolláin, Diarmuid, *Locating Irish Folklore:
   Tradition, Modernity, Identity* (Cork: Cork University
   Press), p. 130

Chapter One

1 Ó Duinn, Seán, *Where Three Streams Meet: Celtic
   Spirituality* (Dublin: Columba Press, 2000), p. 260
2 Referring to the prayers 'Our Father' and 'Hail Mary'
3 He is referring here to the sugar factory where the
   beet was processed
4 Dealing in
5 To dole out
6 An Irish word meaning 'Well!' or 'Indeed'

NOTES

7 Figure of speech approximating to 'well now'
8 It's easy
9 A small shop
10 Shopping
11 Twenty bowls
12 Possibly a derivative of the Irish word 'fuadar' meaning a 'rush' or 'fuss'
13 Old
14 Meaning
15 This was a chemical usually added to laundry water to aid whitening.
16 An Irish word meaning 'bundle'
17 Illicit drinking houses
18 From the Irish 'margadh mór', meaning the big market.
19 I used to see
20 Large wicker baskets
21 I remember a small girl
22 Is
23 By
24 Danaher, Kevin, *The Year in Ireland* (Cork: Mercier Press, 1972), p. 256

Chapter Two

1 Uí Ógáin, Ríonach, 'Aifreann na Gine, Aifreann is Fiche', *Comhar* (Nollaig, 1981), p. 28–30
2 Devil

3 A small field usually adjacent to the house
4 Indeed
5 I remember
6 A small drop of whiskey
7 She is referring here to the scarcity during the years of the Second World War, 1939–45
8 Lights were extinguished during the Second World War due to German air raids
9 Malign hobgoblin
10 Professor Hogan appears to be assuming its complete disappearance in England at the time of writing, but the extent of his research is unknown. He seems unaware, for example, of the Legend of Devils' Dyke from the South Downs area of West Sussex, which is an example of this tradition. In one version of the tale the Devil is digging a trench to flood the weald of Sussex in order to destroy the churches. He never completed the trench as it was said he disturbed a rooster, whose crowing led him to believe it was morning and he fled
11 Uí Ógáin, Ríonach, 'Aifreann na Gine, Aifreann is Fiche,' *Comhar* (Nollaig 1981), p. 30
12 A comprehensive account of customs and beliefs associated with St Bridget can be found in Ó Duinn, Seán, *Gnás na Féile Bríde*, (Baile Átha Cliath, FÁS: 2002)
13 About
14 One
15 A sack of potatoes

16 An island off the coast of County Donegal

Chapter Three

1 Leaving
2 Horse and cart
3 Sip
4 Little bit
5 From the Irish verb crústaigh meaning to pelt
6 This act also included the closing of pubs on Good
   Friday and St Patrick's Day. The ban on pubs opening
   on St Patrick's Day was repealed in 1961
7 A gambling game in which the player who manages to
   throw a coin closest to a mark gets to toss all the coins,
   winning those that land with the head up
8 I was unable to locate a full description of this game
9 One
10 White-coloured traditional woollen sweater
11 Tea
12 Irish word for hurley stick
13 Hurling ball

Chapter Four

1 De Bhaldraithe, Tomás (ed.), *Cín Lae Amhlaoibh*
   (Baile Átha Cliath: An Clóchomhar, 1982), p. 52

2 This contradicts the well-known version which has St Stephen being betrayed
3 From the Irish word bacach meaning beggar or tramp
4 Happening
5 Irish word meaning treasurer
6 Pronounced 'trate'
7 Danaher, Kevin, *The Year in Ireland* (Cork: Mercier Press, 1972), p. 250

Chapter Five

1 see Ó Coigligh, Ciarán, *Raiftearaí: Amhráin agus Dánta* (Dublin, An Clóchomhar, 1987), p. 44
2 *The Year in Ireland*, p. 259
3 Ibid., p. 259
4 Old
5 From feeding the animals
6 Meaning
7 Shamrock
8 The collector Seán McGrath added the following note: Seamróg was preserved in a jam jar from the previous St Patrick's Day, and the palm used for this triple burning was the bit that was usually on the picture of the Sacred Heart or other Holy picture on Palm Sunday. This particular custom was observed in at least three houses in the town of Kilrush this year, and the writer witnessed it in one, namely that of Mr Tone O'Dea

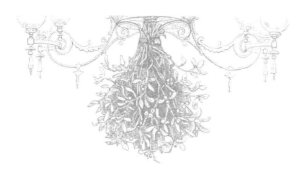

Acknowledgements

Firstly, I'd like to pay tribute to all the collectors, contributors and informants whose work in the collection of Irish folklore has led to the preservation of a rich heritage for future generations.

I am very grateful to all of the following for their help and assistance: All the staff of the Library, Mary Immaculate College, Limerick, with a special thanks to Elizabeth Brosnahan and Marian Fogarty; Beth Amphlett and the staff of The History Press, Ireland; Dr Críostóir Mac Cárthaigh and Professor Ríonach Uí Ógáin, National Folklore Collection, University College, Dublin; Máire Ní Neachtain, Head of the Irish Department, Mary Immaculate College, Limerick; Dr Maria Beville, Limerick Institute of Technology; Dr Tracy Fahey, Limerick School of Art & Design, LIT.

AN IRISH CHRISTMAS

I am very grateful to Myra O'Reilly who provided the illustrations which accompany the text.

Thanks to Dale Healy and Ciara Healy for their assistance.

A special thanks to my wife, June Healy, and my father, Eamon Newman, for their help and support.